To Cindy,

When the
Lights Go Out

Tell a spooky tale!

Margaret Read MacDonald

Tell-a-Spooky-Tale

ABOUT THE AUTHOR:

Margaret Read MacDonald received her Ph.D. in folklore from Indiana University. In addition to her duties as children's librarian in the King County Library System in Seattle, Washington, she travels to many states to conduct courses in storytelling. Her books include *Storyteller's Sourcebook, Twenty Tellable Tales, When the Lights Go Out, Booksharing,* and *The Skit Book.*

When the Lights Go Out

Twenty Scary Tales to Tell

By Margaret Read MacDonald

Illustrations by Roxane Murphy

THE H. W. WILSON COMPANY
1988

Second Printing 1991

First Paperback Printing 1991

International Standard Book Number 0-8242-0823-4
(Paperback)

Library of Congress Cataloging-in-Publication Data

MacDonald, Margaret Read, 1940-
    When the lights go out : twenty scary tales to tell / by Margaret
Read MacDonald ; illustrations by Roxane Murphy.
      p. cm.
    Bibliography: p.
    Summary: Designed primarily as a collection of scary fare for
adults to tell elementary-age children, the tales may be read and
some even told by children. Also contains notes on the stories.
    ISBN 0-8242-0770-X
    1. Storytelling. 2. Libraries, Children's — Activity programs.
3. Children's stories. 4. Horror tales. [1. Folklore. 2. Horror
stories. 3. Storytelling.]   I. Murphy, Roxane, ill.
II. Title.
Z718.3.M24 1988   027.62'51 — dc 19   88-14197 **CIP** **AC**

For Matthew, Monica, Martha, Peter, Bobby, and Eddie Hicks,
who, after twenty years of listening,
still want to hear "Little Dog Turpie" one more time

CONTENTS

PART I: TALES

NOT TOO SCARY

For other not-too-scary stories, see "The Tale of a Black Cat" (page 155), "The Strange Visitor" (page 133), "Who Lives in the Skull?" (page 143), "Witches' Brew" (page 159), and "Let's Go on a Ghost Hunt!" (page 148).

SCARY IN THE DARK

Other stories that can be scary in the dark are "Totanguak" (page 118), "Sam'l" (page 109) and "The Red Silk Handkerchief" (page 129). "The Strange Visitor" (page 133) and "Witches' Brew" (page 159) can be frightening if told for a scary effect.

GROSS STUFF

Also see "Witches' Brew" (page 159) and all of the Scary in the Dark stories.

JUMP TALES (to make your audience jump at the end)

TALES TO ACT OUT

TALES TO DRAW OR STIR UP

PART II: SOURCES

ADDITIONAL GUIDELINES
TO HELP YOU SELECT TALES

Tales with no direct reference to the supernatural:

"Old Ben" (page 104)
"The Cat with the Beckoning Paw" (page 115)
"Who Lives in the Skull?" (page 143)
"Let's Go on a Ghost Hunt!" (page 148)
    (Make it a bear hunt)
"The Tale of a Black Cat" (page 155)

Tales with nonwestern witches, devils, or ghosts:

"Little Buttercup"—troll antagonist (page 7)
"The Hobyahs"—fierce beasts (page 96)
"Totanguak"—an Eskimo spirit of string figures (page 118)

Tales with audience participation possibilities:

"Little Buttercup" (page 7)
"The Wee Little Tyke" (page 21)
"The Great Red Cat" (page 47)
"The Conjure Wives" (page 79)
"The Hobyahs" (page 96)
"The Strange Visitor" (page 133)
"Who Lives in the Skull?" (page 143)
"Let's Go on a Ghost Hunt!" (page 148)
"The Tale of a Black Cat" (page 155)
"Witches' Brew" (page 159)

On repeated tellings, the audience may be encouraged to join in re-
frains on "The Wizard Clip" (page 61), "The Tinker and the Ghost"
(page 69), and "The Red Silk Handkerchief" (page 129), but initial
tellings of those tales will be more effective without audience
participation.

INTRODUCTION

When my storytelling collection *Twenty Tellable Tales* was published in 1986, I called a cousin who teaches second grade in Philadelphia to tell her about the book. She misunderstood the title. "*Twenty Terrible Tales!*" she exclaimed. "What a marvelous idea—the kids will love it!" That's what inspired me to pull out my Halloween file and begin looking for the twenty "terrible" tales presented in *When the Lights Go Out*. Actually, not all the tales I've chosen for this collection *are* so terrible. Included are several mild tales for primary and even preschool audiences, and much of my favorite scary fare is simply not all that frightening. There are a few selections, though, that I consider passably horrifying. The contents (page vi) will guide you to the different types of tales, from the not very frightening to stories that make you jump.

This collection is *not* primarily a Halloween sourcebook, though around that holiday it may prove indispensable for those with avid story listeners to satisfy. I've found the Halloween season to be the time of year when elementary-age children are most eager to hear stories. I think you will find these tales entertaining and meaningful in any season. Many of them deal with themes that children need to hear.

1

Using Scary Stories with Children

Folktales are just that—tales of the folk. They have grown out of centuries of human thought and encompass a wide array of emotions and impulses, not all of them pleasant. Folktales reveal, in fact, that the sentiments of the "folk" who originated them were generally on the side of vengeance rather than mercy. Often folktale characters extract a somewhat rough justice. The Grimm's witch, to take only one example, is put in red-hot iron shoes and made to dance until she dies.

Some people object to the violence in folktales, but it is important to realize that it serves a real purpose. As psychologist Bruno Bettelheim points out, children benefit from seeing their own violent and antisocial feelings acted out on the safe stage of a "make-believe" story. He emphasizes that children need to learn that antagonistic thoughts are part of the human condition, and that sometimes feeling angry does not mean one is "bad" or abnormal.

Just as children can learn to deal with their anger through folktales, so too they are able to examine their fears. Tale protagonists who conquer their fears can prove helpful models for children struggling to come to terms with their own anxieties. Folktales offer a safe realm in which children may experience—and overcome—danger. The child who endures a scary tale shares the triumph of the hero or heroine.

Keep in mind that the degree of scariness in a tale depends a lot on the way it is told. "The Hobyahs" (page 96), for instance, can be a terrifying story or a humorous word play, depending on the telling. Obviously some tales are simply too scary for some children, no matter how they are told. This is something about which the teller must remain sensitive.

About the Tale Texts

These tale texts were *told* into shape. They are creations of the tongue, not the pen. Every Halloween I invite scouts, school classes, any group that wants to come, to sign up for a storytime at the library. I book two sessions each afternoon for the two weeks prior to Halloween. This gives a large number of elementary-age listeners a storytelling experience they seem not to forget. (The small, dark "spooky room" where we huddle together for our stories helps make the tellings memorable.) By the end of my two-week Halloween telling stint, I have told my set of tales at least twenty times. I am a firm believer in the value of repeated tellings as a tale polishing device. The somewhat shaky story of the first Monday's telling has usually formed itself into an emerging gem by the second Friday. This is why I say that these tales have been told, not written, into shape.

Once the tale is working well and settling into a form that bears repeating, I tape myself during a performance. I then transcribe the tape and edit the transcription into texts like those you find here.

About the Tale Notes

For each tale I have written brief comments about my own tellings, making suggestions you might find useful. Every teller develops a unique style, however, so use my hints as guides, not rules. I discuss my own theories about learning and telling stories in *Twenty Tellable Tales* (H. W. Wilson, 1986); if you are a beginning teller, you may find it helpful to consult that book.

Each tale is also accompanied by a note about its origins and by suggestions for finding variants of the story. It is fascinating to begin tracking down variants. Compare the Norwegian "Little Buttercup" with its British variant "Little Jip" or its Armenian cousin "Aram and the Dervish." This can make an interesting activity for your students and leads naturally to discussions about cultural differences as well as literary matters of plot, structure, and sequencing. What are the bare bones that each variant contains? How are the tales dressed differently in various cultures?

The tale notes refer to Stith Thompson's *Motif-Index of Folk Literature* classification—Motif numbers—and to Antti Aarne and Stith Thompson's *The Types of the Folktale* classification—Type numbers. You could think of these as the Dewey Decimal system for folktales. Each tale discovered anywhere in the world is given a type number and each part of a tale is given a motif number. Folklorists use these numbers to talk to each other. When the German folklorist mentions Type 327C, the Norwegian folklorist might think of "Little Buttercup" and the British folklorist might recall "Little Jip," both variants of Type 327C.

It is useful for you to know about motif and type numbers, because they enable you to search for variants of a tale, should you decide to do a little folklore research of your own. Story collections prepared by folktale scholars usually include keys to the motifs and types included in that collection. The Thompson Motif Index and the Aarne-Thompson Type Index give access to a vast body of scholarly material. To provide this kind of access to children's collections, I compiled *The Storyteller's Sourcebook: A Subject, Title, and Motif-Index to Folklore Collections for Children* (Gale/Neal-Schuman, 1982). It indexes over 500 children's folktale collections. You can begin your search with a story title, a subject, or a motif number. The tale notes here will refer frequently to this source as well.

A Note for Teachers and Librarians

You will find that the ethnopoetic format of these tales—lines are arranged to correspond with oral phrasing, and emphasis is indicated by simple reading cues—makes them easy for you to learn and tell. But please do not think of this as a book just for adult storytellers: this same format also makes the tales very readable for children. I realized this while watching two fourth-grade girls read aloud from *Twenty Tellable Tales* in a school library. Their pacing and intonation were perfect and the reading was quite entertaining, even though they were reading the material without any previous preparation. The generous line spacing and ethnopoetic format significantly increase a child's chance of success when reading aloud. This format also makes the stories more approachable for the reluctant or unsure reader. One teacher I know follows her telling of these tales by passing out copies of them, so members of her reading group can then read the stories to themselves. The material would also work well as reader's theater. Just assign parts and have the children enact their own read-aloud plays.

Finally, some of the easier stories in both *Twenty Tellable Tales* and *When the Lights Go Out* are perfect for the child who is just beginning to experiment with the storyteller's art. So do not hide this collection on your professional materials shelf, but put it in the hands of your students so that they may continue enjoying the tales after storytime has ended.

Part I: Tales

LITTLE BUTTERCUP

Once there was a little boy
who was so plump and fat that his mother called him
Little Buttercup.

One day when his mother was kneading bread
the DOG began to bark!

> "Run quick, Little Buttercup,
> and see why Goldtooth the Dog is barking,"
> said his mother.

So Buttercup ran out.

> "Oh Mother Mother . . .

it's the Troll Hag coming over the hill
with her head under her arm
and a bag on her back!"

"Quick Little Buttercup . . .
hide beneath my breadboard.
And when she comes in . . .
don't make a peep."

So Little Buttercup hid under his mother's breadboard.

IN came the TROLL HAG.

"Good day," said the old hag,
"where's Little Buttercup today?"

"Oh he's out with his father . . .
hunting pigeons,"
said Buttercup's mother.

"What a pity.
I had a little silver knife
as a present for Little Buttercup.
It's a pity he's not here."

When Little Buttercup heard that
he could not contain himself.

"Oh Pip Pip . . .
here I am!" he called.

And out he came from under the breadboard.

"Here I am!
Where's my little silver knife?"

"Oh it's right here in my bag,"
said the Troll Hag.
"Just crawl inside and fetch it out."

So that foolish Little Buttercup
crawled into the witch's bag
to get his little silver knife.

As soon as he was in the bag
the Troll Hag threw the bag over her shoulder
and tromped off over the hill
chanting,

      "Buttercup Soup
      Buttercup Soup
      Buttercup Soup
      Buttercup Soup."

After a while she became tired
and sat down under a tree to rest.

      "Tell me, Little Buttercup . . .
      how far is it off to Snoring?"
      (This troll hag lived at Snoring.)

      "Oh it's a long way to Snoring,"
      said Little Buttercup,
      "I think five or six miles."

"Then I'd better have a nap,"
said the Troll Hag.
And she lay down and fell asleep.

While she slept,
Buttercup took his little silver knife
and cut a hole in the bag.
He crept out.
Buttercup found a heavy fir tree root.
He put the root in the bag in his place.
Then Buttercup ran away home to his mother.

When the Troll Hag reached home
she dumped out her bag
and found only a fir tree root!

Next day
Buttercup's mother was kneading her bread
when the DOG began to bark!

"Run quick, Little Buttercup,
and see why Goldtooth the Dog is barking,"
said his mother.

Little Buttercup ran out.

"Oh Mother Mother . . .
it's the Troll Hag coming over the hill
with her head under her arm
and a bag on her back."

"Quick, Little Buttercup . . .
hide beneath my breadboard.
And when she comes in . . .
don't make a peep."

So Little Buttercup hid under his mother's breadboard.

IN came the TROLL HAG.

"Good day," said the old hag,
"where's Little Buttercup today?"

"Oh he's out with his father . . .
hunting wild ducks."

"What a pity.
I had a little silver fork in my bag
as a present for Little Buttercup.
It's a pity he's not here."

When Little Buttercup heard this
he could not contain himself.

"Oh Pip Pip . . .
here I am!" he called.

And out he came from under the breadboard.

"Here I am!
Where's my little silver fork?"

"It's right here in my bag,"
said the Troll Hag.
"Just crawl inside and fetch it out."

So that foolish Little Buttercup
crawled into the witch's bag
to get his little silver fork.

As soon as he was in the bag
the Troll Hag threw the bag over her shoulder
and tromped off over the hill
chanting,

"Buttercup Soup
Buttercup Soup
Buttercup Soup
Buttercup Soup."

After a while she began to feel tired
and sat down under a tree to rest.

"Tell me, Little Buttercup . . .
how far is it off to Snoring?"

"Ohhhh it's a long way to Snoring,"
said Little Buttercup,
"I think ten or eleven miles."

"Then I'd better have a nap,"
said the Troll Hag.

And she lay down and fell asleep.

While she slept,
Buttercup took his little silver fork,
and poked a hole through the bag.
Buttercup found a large stone.
He put the stone in the bag in his place.
Then Little Buttercup ran away home to his mother.

When the Troll Hag reached home
she dumped out her bag
and found a great heavy stone!

Next morning
Buttercup's mother was kneading her bread
when the DOG began to bark!

      "Run quick, Little Buttercup,
      and see why Goldtooth the Dog is barking,"
      said his mother.

So Buttercup ran out.

      "Oh Mother Mother . . .
      it's the Troll Hag coming over the hill
      with her head under her arm
      and a bag on her back!"

      "Quick Little Buttercup . . .
      hide beneath my breadboard.
      And when she comes in . . .
      don't make a peep."

So Little Buttercup hid under his mother's breadboard.

IN came the TROLL HAG.

"Good day," said the old hag.
"Where's Little Buttercup today?"

"Oh he's out with his father . . .
hunting ptarmigan."

"What a pity.
I had a little silver spoon
as a present for Little Buttercup.
It's a pity he's not here."

When Little Buttercup heard that . . .
that foolish boy could not contain himself.

"Oh Pip Pip . . .
here I am!" he called.

And out he came from under the breadboard.

"Here I am!
Where's my little silver spoon?"

"Oh it's right here in my bag,"
said the Troll Hag.
"Just crawl inside and fetch it out."

So Little Buttercup
crawled into the troll hag's bag
to get his little silver spoon.

As soon as Buttercup was in the bag
the Troll Hag threw the bag over her shoulder
and tromped off over the hill
chanting,

> "Buttercup Soup
> Buttercup Soup
> Buttercup Soup
> Buttercup Soup."

After a while she became tired
and sat down under a tree to rest.

> "Tell me, Little Buttercup . . .
> how far is it off to Snoring?"

> "Ohhhh it's a long way to Snoring,"
> said Little Buttercup,
> "I think fifteen or twenty miles."

> "Then I'd better have a nap,"
> said the Troll Hag.

And she started to lie down . . .

> "Twenty miles!!
> But that's impossible!"

said the witch.
"You have cheated me twice, Little Buttercup.
But not THIS time."

And she threw the bag over her back once more
and tromped off over the hills
chanting,

> "Buttercup Soup
> Buttercup Soup
> Buttercup Soup
> Buttercup Soup."

When the Troll Hag reached her home
she called her Troll Daughter.

> "Here's Little Buttercup come for dinner.
> You must chop off his head
> and stew him in the pot
> while I go invite the guests."

When the Troll Hag was gone
the Troll Daughter took Buttercup to the chopping block.
But how to chop off his head?
She didn't know.
She held the ax this way . . .
and that way . . .
Still she seemed not to know how to chop.

> "Would you like me to show you how?"
> said Little Buttercup.

"It's really quite simple.
Just put your head right here
and hand me the ax."

So Little Buttercup chopped off the head of the Troll Daughter
and put her into the stew pot.

Then Little Buttercup climbed up onto the chimney
and waited for the Troll Hag to come home.
And he carried up with him the fir root and the large stone.

When the Troll Hag came home
she went straight to her stew pot and tasted the broth.

"Mmmm Mmmm . . .
Good by my troth
Buttercup BROTH,"
said the Troll Hag.

But Little Buttercup called down the chimney,
"Good by my troth
TROLL broth!"

Then the Troll Hag tasted the soup again.

"Mmmm Mmmm . . .
Good by my troth
Buttercup BROTH!"

But Little Buttercup called down the chimney,
"Good by my troth
TROLL broth!"

17

A third time the Troll Hag tasted the soup.

> "Mmmm Mmmm . . .
> Good by my troth
> Buttercup BROTH!"

Then she looked up the chimney
to see if the echo would come again.
So Little Buttercup threw the stone and the fir root
right down the chimney
calling,
> "Good by my troth
> TROLL broth!!!"

And the heavy stone and the fir root knocked that Troll Hag
right into the pot herself.

Little Buttercup called out,
> "Good by my troth
> It's DOUBLE troll broth!"

Then he took his little silver knife
and his little silver fork
and his little silver spoon
and went along home to his mother.

NOTES ON TELLING

There is a great deal of dialogue in this story. You need not work up different
voices for the characters, but you can convey their personalities through into-

nation and pacing. Since the story repeats itself three times, you need to vary the pacing on the second and third renditions. Make the tale suspenseful by pausing . . . will Little Buttercup be so foolish again? Give the audience a moment to wonder before he begins his "Pip Pip . . . here I am!" The children will enjoy joining you in the troll hag's "Buttercup Soup" chant.

As a follow-up activity you might want to let a group of children adapt this as a puppet play. It lends itself well to that medium. But be certain you are comfortable with Buttercup's violent destruction of the trolls at the story's end before you try to use this tale. I recommend that you read Sigrid Undset's version of this tale for its flavor before you tell it (*see* Comparative Notes).

COMPARATIVE NOTES

Tales in which a devil or witch carries the hero home in a bag are plentiful in European folklore. The tale is Type 327C *The Devil (Witch) Carries the Hero Home in a Sack. The wife or daughter are to cook him, but are thrown into the oven themselves.* The Aarne-Thompson index, *Types of the Folktale*, lists variants as French, Finnish-Swedish, Lithuanian, Norwegian, Faroe Islands, Icelandic, English, Irish, Catalan, Dutch, Flemish, Walloon, German, Italian, Hungarian, San Marino, Slovenian, Serbo-Croatian, Polish, Russian, Turkish, English-American, and African.

The "Little Buttercup" variant of this tale was collected by the nineteenth century folklorists Peter Christen Asbjørnsen and Jørgen Moe. It has been omitted from most of the children's editions of their work published in the United States, but it does appear in the 1960 Viking edition of their *Norwegian Folk Tales* (p. 97–101). This edition should be consulted for its informative forward about the collecting efforts of Asbjørnsen and Moe, and for its extraordinary illustrations taken from the 1879 and 1888 Norwegian editions illustrated by Erik Werenstold and Theodor Kittelsen. Sigrid Undset includes the tale in her *True and Untrue and Other Norse Tales* (p. 156–160), and her text has been included in Phyllis Fenner's *Giants, Witches, and a Dragon or Two* (p. 108–114) and in Elizabeth Hoke's *Witches, Witches, Witches* (p. 32–36).

In my *Storyteller's Sourcebook* "Little Buttercup" is cited under K526 *Captor's bag filled with animals or objects while captive escapes.* Two variants from England are listed: Eileen Colwell's "Jack Buttermilk" in *Round About and Long Ago* (p. 87–89) and Ruth Manning-Sanders' "Little Jip" in *A Book of Ghosts and Goblins* (p. 74–79). Both are quite similar to "Little Buttercup," but lack the delightful mother-breadboard motif. A third related tale that is available in children's collections is "Aram and the Dervish," an Armenian tale in Virginia Tashjian's *Three Apples Fell from Heaven* (p. 16–21).

This tale also includes Motif G526 *Ogre deceived by feigned ignorance of hero. Hero must be shown how to get into oven (or the like). Ogre shows him and permits self to be burned* and Type 1121 *Ogre's wife burned in his own oven.*

THE WEE LITTLE TYKE

There was a farm where everything had gone wrong.
Old Witch Nanny had put a charm on them.

Old Witch Nanny said to the gate,
    "Let no one from this household pass."
So no one could go out to the fields to tend the sheep.

Old Witch Nanny said to the henhouse door,
    "Let no one from this household pass."
So no one could tend to the hens.

Old Witch Nanny said to the well,
    "Let no one from this household draw water."
So the family had no water to make their porridge.

Mother fretted in the house,
Father and Brother wandered about the farmyard wondering
what to do,
and Little Girl went down the road to fetch some water.

When she reached the river
she found some people trying to drown a little black dog.
He was a wee little tyke and all scruffy.

> "He's smaller than a house cat," they said.
> "He's no good as a guard dog.
> He's even too small for a house dog.
> And he's terrible scruffy.
> We might as well drown him."

Little Girl asked them to give *her* the Wee Little Tyke.
> "I don't mind if he's small and scruffy," she said.
> "I can love him anyway."

So she brought the Wee Little Tyke home.
The mother began to scold,
> "There's no water for the porridge.
> The well's bewitched.
> He'll only die of thirst like the rest of us."

But the Wee Little Tyke spoke up.
> "WOOF! WOOF! WOOF!
> Not if I'M about!
> Let ME take care of this!"

Then the farmer came in.

"I can't get to my sheep," he said.
"The gate's bewitched.
The foxes are after the sheep and I can't get to them."

"WOOF! WOOF! WOOF!
Not if I'M about," said the Wee Little Tyke.
"Let ME take care of this!"

The brother came in.
"The hens are bewitched.
I can't get in the henhouse door.
And the hens won't lay an egg."

Then the Wee Little Tyke spoke up.
"WOOF! WOOF! WOOF!
Not if I'M about.
Let ME take care of this."

"YOU?" said the mother.
"You're no bigger than a house cat!"

"YOU?" said the father.
"You're too small for a guard dog."

"YOU?" said the brother.
"You're too *scruffy*."

But the Little Girl picked him up and hugged him.
"YOU!" said the Little Girl.
"*Would* you?
Could you?"

"I *would*
and what's more I WILL!"
said the Wee Little Tyke.

And out the door he went.

"He can't get through any more than we can," said the
farmer.

But he had.

"You can't pass," said the gate.
"Old Witch Nanny laid a spell on me.
No one from this household may pass."

"Oh but I don't live here *yet*," said the Wee Little Tyke.

And he went right through.

He rounded up all the sheep
and brought them into the sheepfold
safe from the foxes.

Then the Wee Little Tyke went to the henhouse.
"You can't pass," said the henhouse door.
"Old Witch Nanny put a spell on me.
No one from this household may pass."

"Oh but I don't live here *yet*," said the Wee Little Tyke.

And he went into the henhouse and settled each hen on her nest.
He said to them,

"I'll bring you a drink of water.
And then you can each lay an egg for me."

Then the Wee Little Tyke went down to the well.
"You can't draw water here," said the well.
"Old Witch Nanny put a spell on me.
No one from this household may draw water."

"Oh I don't live here *yet*," said the Wee Little Tyke.
And he drew water
and the mother made porridge for their supper.

"What a wonderful little dog!" said the Little Girl.
"*Now* may we keep him?"

"But I'm not done *yet*," said the Wee Little Tyke.
For down the road at that very moment
came Old Witch Nanny.

"Let me out! Let me out!" said the Wee Little Tyke.
"Let *me* take care of her."

So they let the Wee Little Tyke out.

Old Witch Nanny came into the farmyard.
She began to walk widdershins* all around the house.

"This *widdershins* magic will hold them fast," she cackled.

"WOOF WOOF WOOF!

*counterclockwise

25

Your magic won't work!" said the Wee Little Tyke,
"because I've walked behind you backwards
and scratched your footsteps out all the way!"

"WHAT'S THAT?" screeched Old Witch Nanny.

And she turned around so fast that she dropped her broom.

"WOOF WOOF WOOF!
That's clever, that is," said the Wee Little Tyke.

And he stood ACROSS her broom.

Without her broom Old Witch Nanny's magic was no good.
"SCAT! SCAT!" was all she could say.

"WOOF WOOF WOOF!" said the Wee Little Tyke.
"I'm not a house cat.
So don't 'Scat' me!
I can use my teeth as well as bark."

Then that Wee Little Tyke bit and barked
and barked and bit
till Old Witch Nanny
ran and rolled right out of the farmyard
and away down the road.

And they never saw Old Witch Nanny again.

The Little Girl took the Wee Little Tyke into her arms
and said he must live with them forever.

But the Wee Little Tyke said,
> "No. I don't belong."

> "Oh YES," said the family.
> "We all *want* you."

> "But I'm *scruffy*."

> "So is our house cat," said the mother.
> "And we love her."

> "But I'm *too small*."

> "Oh but you've got good teeth," said the farmer.

> "You won't pull my tail?
> Or throw things at me?
> Or step on me when I'm sleeping?"

> "Never! Never!" they all cried.

And the Little Girl brought him a bowl of milk.
When he had lapped it all up he looked around.

> "This is about my size," said the Wee Little Tyke.
And he crawled into one of the farmer's slippers
turned around twice
and went to sleep.

NOTES ON TELLING

This story is enjoyed by preschool and primary-grade children. It makes a rather mild Halloween story, since Old Witch Nanny doesn't seem very scary. Children are caught up in the bold personality of the Wee Little Tyke.

COMPARATIVE NOTES

This story is based on a tale collected by Ruth L. Tongue in *Forgotten Folk Tales* (Manuscript) as reprinted in Katharine M. Briggs, *A Dictionary of British Folk-Tales*, Part B, Folk Legends, Volume 2, p. 674–676. The tale was "told by a visiting minister from near Carlisle in 1912." Ruth L. Tongue includes the tale in her *Forgotten Folk-Tales of the English Counties* (London: Routledge & Kegan Paul, 1970, p. 42–44). She notes that "tyke" is a north-country word for a dog. She lists this as a Northumberland tale from near the Scottish border. The tale is also available in a picturebook by Marcia Sewell, *The Wee Little Tyke: An English Folktale* (New York: Atheneum, 1979).

The tale contains motifs B421 *Helpful dog*; D2080 *Magic used against property*; D1791.2 *Withershins circuit for ill-luck*; and G275.2 *Witch overcome by helpful dog of hero*; among others.

LOOKING FOR HOME

Here's an old tale from Luccombe village in England.

There was a queer old chap kept hanging round the village one year.
Folks did see him nighttimes kind of glowing-like in the dark.
He'd come round in noontime too.
But folks were afraid to speak to him,
his clothes were so peculiar and old-fashioned.

One noontime the old fellow came up to a farm door
where a kind old granny lived.
The granny just couldn't bear to see his sorrow.
So she ups and speaks to him . . .
just like the priest had taught her.
Says,

"In the name of the Lord why troublest thou me?"
Says, "You poor unhappy soul,
come tell I."

And the old grey ghost he says,
     "Where be my mill then?
     And my son's cottage by the oak grove?
     There be a stone mill by the river,
     and no cottage,
     and only one aged old oak."

Then the granny she saw the rights of it.
     "Be the church still there?" she asks.

     "They've got a new stone church since I went to market
         this morning.
     I did promise my wife Bet I wouldn't stay late.
     Where be my dear old wife?"

Then Granny saw how it was.
This poor old soul had been held overlong by the fairy folk . . .
or the Devil himself perhaps . . .
His time had passed long ago
and he could not get back to his own time.

Then Granny asked him,
     "WHO did you meet on the road home from market?"

     "Some queer sort of chap, I met.
     We got to wagering games and telling stories.
     He did want me to stay longer

but I told him my old wife Bet would be waiting.
Where be my dear wife?"

And then, they say
there was a light.
And a wind that smelled sweet as a primrose garden
and a voice like a thrush in song said,

"Come home now, my dear.
You don't belong down there no more.
Come on home."

And the sad old ghost gave a beautiful smile
and he vanished clean away.

NOTES ON TELLING

Ghosts, after all, have their own sad tales to tell. I couldn't resist including this one ghost tale that is not terrible at all. The archaic language seems important to the atmosphere of this tale. If it is too awkward for easy telling, just read it aloud. This one will lose its effect if you try to retell it in contemporary English. If you like the language, you may want to consult the even more archaic original in Katharine Brigg's *Dictionary of British Folk-Tales* (*see* Comparative Notes).

COMPARATIVE NOTES

This story is retold from Katharine Briggs, *A Dictionary of British Folk-Tales*, Part A, Volume 1 (Bloomington: Indiana University Press, 1970, p. 426–427). It was collected by Ruth L. Tongue from "a very old farmer in 1929, Horner, Luccombe, and Porlock area." Briggs cites the tale as Type 471 A *The Monk and the Bird,* and refers to Motif F377 *Supernatural lapse of time in fairyland,* and E545.19.2 *Proper way of addressing ghosts,* among others.

This tale is, of course, related to such well-known stories as Rip Van Winkle (D1960.1) and Urashima Taro (F420.6.1.3.1). This tale is unusual in that the character appears as a ghost rather than as a living human misplaced in time. For other elapsed-time tales, see MacDonald's *Storyteller's Sourcebook* D1890; D1960.1; D2011; F372.2.2; F377; F378.1; F420.6.1.3.1; and G312.8.

WICKED JOHN AND THE DEVIL

One time
there was an old man.
His name was Wicked John.

He was the meanest old man you ever saw in your life.
He was just plain cussed mean.
He wouldn't do nothin' good for nobody.

Wicked John lived in a log cabin way up in the hills.
He had a blacksmith shop up there.

One night Wicked John was sittin' down to the supper table
when there come a knockin' at the door.

Wicked John went to the door
and there was an old man . . .
all hunkered over . . .
had a long white beard . . .
said,
> "Wicked John . . . give me a bite to eat."

Well Wicked John . . .
you know how mean he was . . .
he wouldn't do nothin' good for nobody . . .
but that night somethin' peculiar come over him.
He said, "All right Grandpop . . .
> I'll give you a bite to eat."

He brought that old man in . . .
set him down at the table . . .
and give him a big plate of cornbread and greens and hambone.

Now when he finished eatin'
that old man started gettin' up from the table.
He started gettin' up . . .
and gettin' up . . .
And he wasn't any old man at ALL.

He was a great big *husky* feller.
He had a long white beard all right.
And a long white robe clear down to the ground.
And a bunch of *gold keys* . . . on a chain around his waist.

Says,
> "Wicked John . . . I reckon you know who I am NOW."

Wicked John didn't know who he was.

Says,

> "I am *Saint Peter.*
> I guard the pearly gates up in heaven.
> Once a year I come down and wander around the earth.
> And if anybody is good to me . . .
> I give them THREE WISHES.
>
> Now I know what a mean old man you've been all your life.
> But you *were* good to *me.*
> So I've got to give you *three wishes.*
>
> Now what do you want to wish for?"

Wicked John started looking around that cabin.
> "Let me see . . . "
And he was thinkin' *mean.*

> "I know!
> See that rocking chair over there?
> That's *my* chair.
> Every night when I'm tired, I want to sit down in that chair
>   and rest.
> But every time I go to sit in that chair
> there's somebody else *a-sittin'* in it.
>
> I want you to make it . . .
> so that if anybody sits in my chair . . .
> for any reason at *all* . . .

that chair will GRAB hold of them
and rock back and forth . . . back and forth . . .
and not STOP
till *I* say, 'Stop CHAIR!'"

"Laws, that's a TERRIBLE wish,"
said Saint Peter.
"But I've got to give it to you.
Now what's your next wish?"

Wicked John started looking around that cabin.
And he was still thinkin' *mean*.

"Let me see . . .
That HAMMER.
See that hammer over there?
That's MY hammer.
I use that to make these horseshoes.
But those fool kids come in here . . .
carry off my hammer . . .
take it out in the road bustin' up rocks with it . . .
I can't find it for nothin'.

I want you to make it . . .
so if anybody *touches* my hammer . . .
for any reason at all . . .
that hammer will STICK onto them
and hammer up and down . . . up and down . . .
till *I* say 'Stop HAMMER!'"

"Well that's a mean wish," said Saint Peter.
"But I've got to give it to you."

"Now you've only got one more wish.
You'd better make it a *good* one."

Wicked John started looking around that cabin.
And he was thinkin' as *mean* as ever.

"Let me see . . .
See that thorn bush out that window?
That's MY thorn bush.
It blooms so pretty every spring.
But these here city fellers
come out here to get their horses shoed . . .
they break off a switch here . . .
and break off a switch there . . .
by the end of summer it's just plumb *scraggly*.

Now I want you to make it . . .
so that if *anybody* reaches into my thorn bush . . .
for any reason at all . . .
that thorn bush is going to GRAB them
and pull them down inside
where the prickles is the longest . . .
and PRICKLE THEM HARD!
And not stop
till *I* say 'Stop BUSH!'"

"Law, that's a mean wish!" said Saint Peter.
"You've got your three wishes.
Now I'm a-goin!"

And he went out the door
and he vanished
and was seen no more.

Well Wicked John went on
a-livin' like he'd been livin' before.
And he got meaner every day . . .
and meaner every day . . .
until finally the Old Fellow down below
heard about Wicked John.

He figured it was time for Wicked John to come down
    there to live.

Called his little son,
        said, "Little Devil . . .
        you go on up there and get that man Wicked John.
        Tell him it's time for him to come down HERE to live."

Wicked John was a-workin' on a horseshoe.
He looked up
and there was that Little Devil in the doorway.

Says, "Wicked John . . .
        my Daddy says it's time for you to COME."

Wicked John knew what that Little Devil was there for . . .
and he didn't want to go . . .

Says,
        "Well . . . I don't mind goin' with you Little Devil . . .

but I'm workin' on a horseshoe here.
I'd sure like to finish it before I *go*.
Tell you what . . .
Why don't you just sit down in that CHAIR over there
    . . . and wait a spell."

Little Devil says,
    "Well . . . I don't mind if I DO."

Little Devil sat down in that chair
and that chair FASTENED onto that Little Devil
and began rockin' back and forth . . . back and forth . . .
Little Devil was goin' LAM BANG against the back of that
    chair . . .
yelling "WICKED JOHN! WICKED JOHN!
    Tell this chair to STOP!"

        "If I tell that chair to stop . . .
        are you going to go out that door
        and down that road
        and not come back in these parts no more?"

        "Oh I AM! I AM!
        Just tell this chair to STOP!"

Wicked John said "All right.
    Stop CHAIR."

That Little Devil TORE out of the door
and down that road
and HE didn't come back in those parts no more.

Daddy Devil didn't like that.
He called his next bigger son.

Says, "Little Devil . . .
        You go up there and tell that man Wicked John
        to get on down here
        and no more FOOLISHNESS."

Wicked John was a-workin' on a horseshoe.
He looked up
and there was that Little Devil in the doorway.

Wicked John knew what he was there for
and he sure didn't want to go.

        "Well I don't mind goin' with you, Little Devil . . .
        but I'd sure like to finish this horseshoe here before I go.
        Why don't you grab hold of that hammer . . .
        and lend me a hand."

Little Devil looked around . . .
        "Why I don't mind if I DO . . . "

Grabbed hold of that hammer.

That hammer FASTENED onto that Little Devil
and started hammering up and down . . . up and down . . .
Little Devil was going LAM BANG on the end of that hammer.

        "WICKED JOHN . . . WICKED JOHN . . . !
        Tell this hammer to STOP!"

"If I tell that hammer to stop . . .
are you going to go out that door
and down that road
and not come back any more?"

"Oh I AM! I AM!
Tell this hammer to STOP!"

"All right then.
Stop HAMMER."

That Little Devil TORE out the door . . .
down that road . . .
and HE didn't come back there no more either.

The old Daddy Devil didn't like that.
He figured he'd have to go up there and get Wicked John himself.

Next thing Wicked John knew
there was the OLD BOY HIMSELF in the doorway.
With his horns . . .
and his long tail . . .
and his pitchfork . . .
Had his *hoof* up there on the doorsill . . .

Says, "Wicked John I've come to GET you.
        And I don't want no more of your FOOLISHNESS.
        You're a-comin' with ME."

That Old Devil grabbed Wicked John
and they started in a-fightin'.

A-kickin' and a-scratchin' and a-bitin' . . .
It was PITIFUL.

And the Old Devil . . .
he won.
He grabbed Wicked John by the back of the neck
and shook him . . .
says, "Wicked John . . . I'm a-goin' to teach you a LESSON.
      I'm a-goin' to take you outside
      and get me a SWITCH.
      And I'm a-gonna whup you GOOD."

He dragged Wicked John out the door . . .
and he reached into that *thorn bush*
to get a switch.
That thorn bush GRABBED that Old Devil
PULLED him inside where the prickles was the longest . . .
and prickled him HARD.
And it wouldn't STOP.

      "WICKED JOHN! WICKED JOHN!
      Tell this thorn bush to STOP!"

      "If *I* tell that thorn bush to stop . . .
      are you going to go out that gate . . .
      and down that road . . .
      and not come back in these parts no more?"

      "Oh I AM! I AM!
      Just tell this thorn bush to STOP!"

Wicked John said,
　　"*Stop* BUSH."

That Old Devil TORE out that gate . . .
and down that road . . .
and let me tell you . . .
HE didn't come back in them parts no more EITHER.

Well time went by
and like all men
Wicked John died.

He thought he might as well go up to Heaven.
So he started walkin' up that road . . .
and walkin' up that road . . .
knocked on those Pearly Gates . . .

Saint Peter come out.
　　"Wicked John WHAT are you doin' up HERE?
　　You *know* what a mean old man you've been all your life.
　　You're gonna have to go *down below*."

Wicked John turned around.
Started walkin' down the road . . .
walkin' down the road . . .
to that place down below.

As it was . . .
those two Little Devils that had met him
were playing out in front of the gate.
They looked up the road and saw Wicked John a-comin'.

They ran inside calling,
    "DADDY! DADDY!
    Come BOLT the gate quick!
    That *mean old man's a-comin'!*"

Tha old Daddy Devil ran out.
He slammed the gate
and locked it up tight.

They wouldn't let Wicked John in down THERE either.

Wicked John said,
    "Well what am I gonna DO?
    Where am I gonna GO?"

The old Daddy Devil grabbed a big ball of fire in his tongs
and he *threw* it over the wall to Wicked John.

Says, "Here, Wicked John.
    You go make you a PLACE OF YOUR OWN."

Now sometimes in the night
if you're out in the swamp
you'll see a ball of fire
movin' along the horizon.
Some folks call it will-o'-the-wisp
and some folks call it swamp lightning . . .
but it ain't that at all.
It's just Wicked John
out lookin' for to make him
a PLACE OF HIS OWN.

NOTES ON TELLING

This tale will be enjoyed by junior-high listeners, teens, and adults, as well as by elementary-age children. The story is lengthy and requires considerable effort to learn, but it is a rhythmic tale that will stick with you once you have mastered it. If you like the plot but don't care for the Southern dialect, see some of the many variants listed in my *Storyteller's Sourcebook* for an alternate version.

Pacing is all-important in this story. The first Little Devil should slowly contemplate sitting down . . . "Don't mind if I do," then become increasingly more frantic as he is unable to stop rocking. Wicked John's "All right. *Stop CHAIR*" should be very still and deliberate, a punctuation after the Little Devil's frenzied scene. I let him fold his arms to deliver this line; he is enjoying the scene and in no hurry to stop it.

If the final lines of this tale are delivered slowly, a satisfying chill will fall as the vision of Wicked John, walking forever through foggy nights, ball of fire in hand, descends on the room.

COMPARATIVE NOTES

This tale and its many variants have been favorite fare with U.S. storytellers for years. The best known variant is Richard Chase's retelling in *Grandfather Tales*. My own story began with that version but has changed its shape over the years. I think it is worth including here as an alternative to Chase's somewhat more wordy version. For reading aloud I prefer Chase's variant.

This is Tale Type 330 *The Smith Outwits the Devil*. The Aarne-Thompson type index lists variants as: American, Argentinian, Basque, Chilean, Columbian, Czechoslovakian, Danish, Dominican Republican, Dutch, English-American, Estonian, Finnish, Flemish, Franco-American, French, French Antilles, German, Greek, Hungarian, Indian, Irish, Istrian, Italian, Norwegian, Polish, Puerto Rican, Russian, Scottish, Serbo-Croatian, Slovenian, Spanish, Spanish-American, Swedish, and West Indian Black. The basic theme of Type 330 is: Savior or St. Peter visits smith, smith is given three wishes, sticks to bench, tree, etc., smith is admitted neither to heaven nor hell. This is sometimes accompanied by a "devil pounded in knapsack" motif (K213) in which the Devil is tricked into a bag and then beaten. In a very few tales the smith is said to wander the earth holding a lighted turnip or pumpkin (A1917.1 *Origin of Jack-o'-lantern*).

My *Storyteller's Sourcebook* cites children's editions of this tale from France, Ireland, Norway, Slovenia, the U.S. (Joel Chandler Harris), and Wales under Thompson motif 0565 *Man admitted to neither heaven nor hell*. Of particular interest are variants from Ireland (Seumas MacManus, *Hibernian Nights*, p. 10–24), in which the Tinker of Tamlacht becomes a salmon in the river Erne; a variant from Czechoslovakia (Parker Filmore, *Shepherd's Nosegay*, p. 185–192), in which a shoemaker throws his apron into heaven and sits on "his own property"; and an Italian variant (Moritz Jagendorf, *Priceless Cats*, p. 138–146), in which Padre Ulivo hosts all twelve disciples, later gambles with the Devil, wins many souls, and gets them all into heaven: "Tell the Lord I let all of *his* friends in when he came to *my* house."

THE GREAT RED CAT

Now there was a man by the name of Murdo McTaggart.
A fisherman, he was.
And Murdo would go out fishing *every* night of the year . . .
no matter what.

On All Hallow's Eve
all good men would stay at home
or go to church to pray.
But not Murdo McTaggart.

Down he went to the fishermen's hut
to pull out his nets and his oars and go to sea.

Though the night was dark and stormy,

though the lightning flashed, the thunder rolled,
and the rain came down in torrents on the fishermen's hut . . .
still Murdo worked away at preparing his nets.

Suddenly . . .
he felt that someone . . .
or some *thing* . . .
was standing in the door of the hut.

Murdo turned . . .
and there . . .
was a Great Red CAT
with bright *green* eyes.
So large it was that it almost filled the door of the hut.

And the Great Red Cat
came into the hut
and *grinned*
and showed its sharp white teeth
and HISSED.

The Red Cat sat and *stared*
at Murdo.

And behind it in the doorway
appeared a Great BLACK Cat
with bright RED eyes.

And the Great BLACK Cat came into the hut
and *grinned*
and showed its sharp white teeth
and HISSED.

And the Great Black Cat sat and *stared* . . .
at Murdo.

And behind it in the doorway
appeared a *second* Great Black Cat.
And the second Great Black Cat came into the hut
and grinned
and showed its sharp white teeth
and HISSED.

And the second Great Black Cat sat and *stared*
at Murdo.

And behind it in the doorway appeared a THIRD black cat:
  "HISSS!"

And a FOURTH!
  "HISSS!"

A FIFTH!
  "HISSS!"

AND A SIXTH!
  "HISSS . . . !"

Until TWELVE Great Black Cats sat in the room
in a circle round Murdo McTaggart.
And they STARED
at Murdo
with their bright *red* eyes.

And in the middle
sat the RED cat
with the *green* eyes.

Then *stood* the Great Red Cat.

"Come Friends!
Should we sit here in SILENCE this fine stormy night?
Let us all sing a CORONACH! . . .
For MURDO McTAGGART here."

And the cats began to YOWL . . .

And when the cats had done
the Great Red Cat turned to Murdo.

"Come Murdo!
You'll pay us now?
For the fine CORONACH we have sung you this night?"

"And why should I be paying for a *coronach*," said Murdo.
"And me not even *dead*.
I'll not pay."

"But look round at my friends . . . ,"
said the Great Red Cat.
"See how HUNGRY they look from their singing."

And Murdo looked round the circle
and the Twelve Black Cats all STARED . . .
with their bright red eyes . . .

and the Twelve Black Cats all GRINNED . . .
and showed their sharp white teeth . . .
and . . . HISSED!

And Murdo McTaggart knew he had best find them food.

Then Murdo looked out the door, over the cats' heads . . .
and there in the rain
was the Laird's old sheep,
standing with its back to the wind.

The sheep belonged to the Laird of the land
but Murdo was beyond caring who it belonged to.

       "Why THERE'S your pay!"
And he pointed to the sheep on the hill.

OFF went the cats.
UP the hill
and ONTO the sheep.

And in a moment's work they were back
and sat in a circle round Murdo McTaggart
and *stared* with their bright red eyes.

Behind them on the hill in the rain . . .
lay nothing but . . .
a pile of *bones*.
Licked *clean*.

Then stood the Great Red Cat.
       "Come Friends!

Should we sit here in SILENCE this fine stormy night?
Let us all sing a CORONACH! . . .
For MURDO McTAGGART here."

And the cats began to SING. . . .

And when they had finished their song
the Great Red Cat turned to Murdo.

"Come Murdo!
You'll be paying us now?
For the fine CORONACH we have sung you this night?"

"And why should I be paying for a *coronach?*" said Murdo.
"And me not even *dead*.
I'll *not* pay."

"But Murdo . . . "
said the Great Red Cat,
"look round at my friends . . .
How HUNGRY they look from their singing.
You'd best pay."

Murdo looked round at the Twelve Great Black Cats.
And the Twelve Great Black Cats GRINNED . . .
and showed their sharp white teeth . . .
and . . . HISSED!

And Murdo knew he had best find them their pay.

Murdo looked out the door over the cats' heads
and there in the rain
was the Laird's old bony cow.
Standing on the hillside
with its back to the rain.

"Why THERE'S your pay!"
And he pointed to the cow on the hill.

OFF went the cats.
UP the hill
and ONTO the back of the bony old cow.

And in a moment's work they were back
and sat in a circle round Murdo McTaggart
and *stared* with their bright red eyes.

Behind them on the hill in the rain . . .
lay nothing but . . .
a pile of *bones*.
Picked clean.

Then stood the Great Red Cat.
        "Come now Friends!
        Should we sit here in SILENCE this fine stormy night?
        Let us all sing a CORONACH! . . .
        For MURDO McTAGGART here."

And the cats began to HOWL . . .

And when they had done
the Great Red Cat turned to Murdo.

53

"Come Murdo . . .
You'll pay us now?
For the fine CORONACH we have sung you this night?"

"Now why should I be paying for a *coronach?*" said Murdo.
"And me not even *dead?*
No. I'll not pay."

"Look round at my friends, Murdo . . . "
said the Great Red Cat.
"See how *very* HUNGRY they look from their singing.
I think you'd better *pay.*"

Murdo looked round at the Twelve Great Black Cats.
And the Twelve Black Cats all GRINNED . . .
and showed their sharp white teeth . . .
and . . . HISSED!

And Murdo knew it was his own white bones
that would be lying in a pile soon
here in the fishermen's hut.
For it was his own sweet flesh they were hungering after that night.
He had no doubt of it.

Just then
Murdo saw streaking past the door of the hut . . .
the Laird's great greyhound DOG . . .
swifter than swift . . .
        "Why THERE goes your pay!" he called.
        "AFTER it!"

OFF went the cats.
But the greyhound
hearing them come
RACED away over the moors . . .
with the cats yowling behind.

As soon as they had gone from sight
Murdo hurried from that place
up the road to the village
and safety . . .
but before he could reach the village . . .
BACK CAME THE CATS!
For the greyhound had been too swift for them
and they were angry indeed with Murdo McTaggart.

Murdo could do nothing but climb a tall tree
and cling there for safety.

UP came the cats
and surrounded the tree
with a great . . . HISSING!

The FIRST black cat
began to climb the tree
to bring down Murdo McTaggart.
But when it reached the top of the tree . . .
Murdo drew his dagger . . .
and STABBED the Great Black Cat.
And it fell to the ground.

A SECOND black cat

began to climb the tree
to bring down Murdo McTaggart.
But when it reached the top of the tree . . .
Murdo drew his dagger . . .
and STABBED the Great Black Cat.
And it fell to the ground.

     "HOLD!"
     cried the Great Red Cat.
     "He'll have us all dead at this rate.
     We'll not have him down that way.
     We must bring down the TREE
     and Murdo McTaggart IN it."

The cats surrounded the tree
and began to scrabble at the gravel around the tree roots.
Soon they had unearthed the FIRST great root of the tree.
Then the cats barred their sharp teeth
and they began to GNAW.
And when they had gnawed right through the root . . .
the tree gave a shudder . . .
and leaned to one side.
In the top of the tree
Murdo McTaggart let out a great cry for
     "HELP!"

Far away across the moor
the priest in the chapel paused in his mass.
     "I have heard the cry of a man in need!
     I must GO," said the priest.

But his assistant said,

"No, wait.
It may only be a trick of the wind.
Wait and see if the cry comes again."

So the priest went back to his service.

The cats continued to dig.
Soon they unearthed the SECOND great root of the tree.
They barred their sharp teeth and began to GNAW.
And when that root was broken through . . .
the tree lurched . . .
and leaned to the *other* side . . .
And in the top of the tree
Murdo McTaggart let out a second great cry for
        "HEELLPP!!"

Far away across the moor
the priest in the chapel heard.
        "It IS the cry of a man in need!
        I must go at ONCE!"

And the priest set off across the moor
in the direction of the cry.

The cats had unearthed the LAST great root of the tree.
They barred their teeth . . .
and they began to GNAW . . .
When the last great root had been gnawed through
the tree gave a great SHUDDER . . .
and began to FALL . . . to . . . the . . . ground.

And clinging still in the top of the tree
Murdo McTaggart let out a final great cry for
  "HEEEEELLLPP!!!!"

Up raced the PRIEST
with his flask of holy water!
He sprinkled holy water on the Great Black Cats . . .
"PST! . . ."
"PST! . . ."
"PST! . . ."
 . . . Each cat sputtered and fell to the ground.

The priest DASHED the rest of the holy water
on the Great Red Cat . . .
  "YARLLL!!!"

The Great Red Cat LEAPED into the air
  with a horrid YOWL . . .
  and VANISHED!

Only a dreadful smell of smoke and brimstone
came down all around.

And on the ground by the fallen tree . . .
were not dead cats . . .
but only black cat SKINS.
For these had not been real cats at all.
But only DEMONS in the *skins* of cats.

And the *red* one was AULD CLOOTIE *himself.*
And only the PRIEST
could have saved Murdo McTaggart that fine night.

Never again did Murdo McTaggart go to fish on All Hallow's Eve.
Instead he stayed at home
or went to church to pray,
as all good Scotsmen should.

NOTES ON TELLING

Make your hisses sinister as the cats enter one by one. Let the children join you, if you like, and fill the room with an eerie hissing.

Coach the children in caterwauling, either before you start or briefly during the first episode of the story, and let them provide the "coronach" for Murdo each time the cats wail. Establish a clear cut-off signal to stop the cater-wauling abruptly. This can be very effective. You can also let them join you in Murdo's long, drawn out cries for "Heellpp . . . " Take your time with these cries.

Gather the children close about you for this storytelling and darken the room. This tale can be gleefully eerie in performance.

COMPARATIVE NOTES

This tale is created from Sorche Nic Leodhas's telling in *Twelve Great Black Cats* (p. 3–11). I have restructured the tale and added audience participation aspects. This makes it great fun to perform with a group. For reading aloud pleasure, I recommend that you turn to the lovely retelling of the tale by Sorche Nic Leodhas (pseudonym for Le Clair Louise Gowan).

Sorche Nic Leodhas implies that she has heard her tales from Scottish-American friends and relatives. Joseph Campbell found a variant of this tale embodied in a longer tale of a storyteller forced to tell three tales to save his three sons. The tale "Conall Cra Bhuidhe" was heard from James Wilson, a blind fiddler on Islay. It appears in *Popular Tales of the West Highlands* by J. F. Campbell, V. 1 (Edinburgh: Edmonston and Douglas, 1860; reprinted by Wildwood House, 1983). The portion of the story that corresponds to our tale appears on pages 108–111. Tom Peete Cross, in his *Motif-Index of Early Irish Literature*, lists nine entries under B16.1.4 *Fierce cat*, which he cross-references from G303.3.3.3 *Devil in form of a cat*, indicating that the notion of the devil in the form of a cat is a familiar one in Irish tradition.

The tale is an unusual one. It begins with twelve black cats encircling a lone man late at night, much like the tale "Sop Doll" (page 86) in this collection. However the cats are not neighborhood women in the form of witch cats, as in the "Sop Doll" tale; instead, the Great Red Cat is the Devil and the others are his demons (D142.1 *Devil as cat* and G303.3.3.1.2 *Devil in form of a cat*). The tale includes an unusual motif—the singing of a coronach (dirge) for which the unfortunate victim must pay.

The tale ends with motif R251 *Flight on a tree which ogre tries to cut down*. The victim's three calls for help and the arrival at the last moment of the priest who has heard his calls are very like the actions in B524.1.2 *Dogs rescue fleeing master from tree refuge*. In that tale the hero calls to his dogs three times from his treetop perch, and on the last call they break free and come to rescue him. In my *Storyteller's Sourcebook* several children's editions of the B524.1.2 tale are cited.

THE WIZARD CLIP

It was in 1794
in the Shenandoah Valley of Virginia.
I'll call our victim Squire Jeeves.
His name is known
and his tombstone stands today near Smithfield, Virginia.
But I'd rather not conjure up the names of the dead
unless I want their company.
Squire Jeeves was a hard man,
a man with no religion.

> "No priest nor preacher will ever darken my door," said
> Jeeves.
> "There'll be no religion in this house."

His friends shuddered to hear him talk like that.

It was on a dark night in November that he heard a
knock at his door.

An old man it was,
ill from the cold,
a tailor by profession.
Could he spend the night?

Squire Jeeves gave no charity.
Yes he could spend the night,
but he must make a suit of clothes for Jeeves
before he slept.

So the tailor came in.
Jeeves brought out strong broadcloth he'd been saving for a suit.
The tailor took out his scissors
and began to clip the cloth.
        "Snip snip . . .
        snip snip . . .
        snip snip . . . "

Jeeves went to bed and left him at his work.
All night the tailor's scissors clipped,
        "snip snip . . .
        snip snip . . .
        snip snip . . . "

In the morning Jeeves found the old man
collapsed over the table . . .
the cut pieces of the suit strewn around him.
        "I die," he said.

"This was my last night on this earth.
Hurry and bring the priest.
I must have his blessing before my soul can rest."

Jeeves glowered and turned away.
"No priest nor minister will cross the doorstep of
this house," he said.
"I made that vow and will not break it.
If die you must, then do it.
You'll have no blessing from a priest in this house."

"But then my soul . . . can never rest."
The tailor's eyes clouded.
His scissors lifted
Imploring Jeeves for pity.
They made one final . . . "snip . . . "
His life was over.

The body was laid out,
Jeeves did that much.
And candles lit around it.
But the long night through those candles would not stay lit.
They would burn bright for a while and then . . .
"snip snip . . .
snip snip . . .
snip snip . . . "
The flames would be snipped off
as if by unseen scissors.

Jeeves would light them again

and sit awhile in brightness
but then
      "snip snip . . .
      snip snip . . .
      snip snip . . . "
The candles would snuff out,
the room be plunged in darkness.

Next day the tailor was buried.
But that night, all the night long
a snipping sound was heard out in the yard . . .
circling the house . . . again . . . and again . . .
      "snip snip . . .
      snip snip . . .
      snip snip . . . "

And in the morning . . .
every one of Jeeves' chickens
was lying in the yard . . .
with its head snipped off.

That night the snipping came again.
Round and round the house . . .
      "snip snip . . .
      snip snip . . .
      snip snip . . . "

And in the morning . . .
every one of Jeeves' geese
was lying in the fowlyard . . .
with its head snipped off.

That night again the snipping came.

"Snip snip . . .
snip snip . . .
snip snip . . ."

And in the morning . . .
every one of Jeeves' turkey gobblers
was lying in the yard . . .
with its head snipped off.

It was the next night that the hired man left the back door ajar
when he went to the barn after supper.
Forgot to close it . . .
or left it open on purpose . . .
I don't know.

But that night there was a snipping in the kitchen.
All night it was heard.
"Snip snip . . .
snip snip . . .
snip snip . . ."

And in the morning . . .
the curtains and the dishtowels
were all found snipped to shreds.

Next night those sounds came from the living room.
"Snip snip . . .
snip snip . . .
snip snip . . ."

And in the morning . . .
the carpets and the sofa
were all found snipped to pieces.

Next night the scissors sounded on the stairs.
      "Snip snip . . .
      snip snip . . .
      snip snip . . . "

In the morning . . .
the staircase was slit and scarred
up and down.

It was that night that Squire Jeeves had his dream.
In this dream he climbed a steep hill.
At the top a tall man in black robes waited for him.

      "Only HE can save you," said a voice.
      "Only HE."

Squire Jeeves left his house
with its horrible wizard clippers.
He went into town.
He told everyone of his dream . . .
described the man to all.
It was clear to them.
The man in his dream was the village priest.

So Squire Jeeves at last sought out the priest
and begged him to visit his household.
The priest came.

He sprinkled holy water.
He said a prayer.
He blessed the dead tailor's soul.

Such a whirring and snipping began then!
Round and round the room it snipped.
Then out the door.
Those wizard clippers shot across the field
and plunged themselves into a well.

A well with no bottom, folks say.
It's there to this day.
You may look into the well
but you will see no wizard clippers.
They were laid to rest for good by the priest's blessing.

They only live on in this story . . .
of the Wizard Clip.

NOTES ON TELLING

Hold a pair of shears in your hand and slash them together on the snipping parts rather than speaking. If told in a darkened room, this "snipping" is quite eerie. Give one final snip in the silence at the tale's end.

COMPARATIVE NOTES

This tale is created from a legend recounted in *The Southern Folklore Quarterly* (XXV #4, December 1961, p. 256–260) as "The Wizard Clip: An Old Potomac Legend" by Cecil D. Eby, Jr., and Jack B. Moore. They cite as their sources: H. H. Hardesty, *Historical Hand-Atlas* (Berkeley and Jefferson County edition), Chicago and Toledo: 1882; the Shepherdstown (West Virginia) *Register*, November 8, 1922, republished in Marguerite D. Lee, *Virginia Ghosts* (Richmond, 1930); field notes for the WPA writers series on West Virginia in the possession of Cecil D. Eby; and Robert L. Bates, "Middleway, a Study in Social History," *West Virginia History*, XI (October, 1949).

The motif F473.6.2 *Spirit slashes clothing* is cited in Baughman's *Type and Motif Index of the Folktales of England and North America* as having variants from Scotland, New England, and Indiana.

THE TINKER AND THE GHOST

On a wide plain in Spain
not far from the city of Toledo
there stood a great grey castle.

For many years before our story begins
no soul had ventured near the castle
because the castle was *haunted*.

Every night a thin sad voice
could be heard to *moan* and *wail*
around the castle walls.

And one night of the year
All Hallow's Eve

a strange light would flicker and die . . .
flicker and die . . .
in the castle chimney.

Brave men had tried to rid the castle of its ghost.
But they had all been found the next morning
sitting cold and lifeless
before the fireplace in the Great Hall of the castle.

Our story begins on All Hallow's Eve.
A brave and jolly tinker, whose name was Esteban,
came to the village that lay near the castle.
As he sat in the village square
mending pots and pans,
the women of the village told him about the castle . . .
and about the *ghost*.
The castle's owner had offered *one thousand* golden rials
to any man who could rid the castle of its ghost.

"I will gladly *sleep* there tonight
and keep the dismal spirit *company*,"
said Esteban.
"For I am a brave and jolly tinker
and I fear NOTHING . . .
man OR ghost.

But I like good food and a warm fire.
You must bring me . . .
a dozen fresh eggs . . .
a side of bacon . . .
a flask of wine . . .
and wood for my fire."

The villagers gladly brought him these things.
Esteban loaded his provisions onto his donkey
and set off for the castle.
As he climbed the road to the castle on the hill,
a wind whipped through the trees
and lightning cracked across the sky.

Esteban tethered his donkey in the courtyard
and pushed open the huge doors of the Great Hall of the castle.

A dank and dismal air came from the place.
Spider webs fell across his face.
Bats' wings beat the air high up.
Esteban went straight to the stone fireplace in the Great Hall
and lost no time in building a roaring fire.

Then he felt some better.
He took out his frying pan . . .
cut some bacon . . .
and began to fry his bacon over the fire.

But no sooner had the smell of the bacon gone *up* the
    chimney . . .
than a VOICE came *down* the chimney.

> "OOOOOHHH MEEeee . . .
> OOOOOHHH MEEeee . . .
> LOOK OUT BELOWWW . . .
> I'M *FALLINGGG* . . ."

71

And down the chimney with a *thump*
came a man's LEG.

It was a good enough *leg* all right.
Clothed in half a pair of brown corduroy trousers.
Esteban moved the leg away from the fire so it wouldn't burn
and went right on frying his bacon.

"OOOOOHHH MEEeee . . .
OOOOOHHH MEEeee . . .
LOOK OUT BELOWWW . . .
I'M FALLINGGG . . ."

And down the chimney came a second leg
just like the first.

Esteban moved that leg away from the fire
and began to eat his bacon.
He broke an egg into the frying pan
and put that over the fire.

"OOOOOHHH MEEeee . . .
OOOOOHHH MEEeee . . ."

came the voice again.

"LOOK OUT BELOWWW . . .
I'M FALLINGGG . . ."

"All right!" said Esteban.
"Fall away!
But don't spill my EGGS!"

72

And down the chimney
with a *thump*
came a man's TRUNK,
the middle part of his body.

Esteban moved the trunk away from the fire
and kept right on frying his eggs.

    "OOOOOHHH MEEeee . . .
    OOOOOHHH MEEeee . . . "

came the voice again.

    "LOOK OUT BELOWWW . . .
    I'M FALLINGGG . . . "

And down the chimney with a *thump*
came first one arm
and then the other.

    "Well that leaves only the *HEAD*,"
    said Esteban.
    "I must say I am curious
    to see what that head will look like."

He hadn't long to wait.
For the voice began calling again
louder and shriller than ever.

    "OOOOOHHH MEEeee . . .

OOOOOHHH MEEeee . . .
LOOK OUT BELOWWW . . .
I'M FALLINGGG . . . ."

And down the chimney with a *thump*
came a man's HEAD.

It was a good enough *head*
with dark *burning* eyes
and a long black beard.

At that Esteban took his frying pan from the fire.
And it's a good thing he did.
For before his very eyes
the pieces of that man's body assembled themselves *together* . . .
into a living *man*.
Or I should say . . . *ghost* of a living man.
For it *was* a ghost.

"Good day," said Esteban.
"Would you care for some bacon and eggs?"

"I eat no *food*," said the ghost.
"But I can tell you *this*.
You are the first man to stay *alive*
until I could get my body together again.
The others all died of FRIGHT
before I was half down the chimney.

If you will do as I ask you now
I will make you a rich man.

74

Many years ago I stole three bags of coins
and hid them in the courtyard of this castle.
Thieves followed me
and CUT my body into pieces.
But they did not find the *coins.*"

The ghost led the way into the courtyard.
Under a tree the ghost marked a spot.
"Now DIG!" said the ghost.

"Dig *yourself!* " said Esteban.

And so the *ghost* dug.

Soon he unearthed three bags of coins.
"Here is a bag of *copper* coins.
Give them to the *poor.*

Here is a bag of *silver* coins.
Give them to the *church.*

Here is a bag of *golden* coins.
Keep them for *yourself.*

Will you do as I ask you?"

"I will," said Esteban.

"Then *take my clothing from me* and I may rest,"
said the ghost.

Esteban took the ghost's clothing . . .
and the ghost *vanished*.
His soul could *rest*.

In the morning
the villagers came to carry away Esteban's dead body.
But he was very much alive
eating the last of his bacon and eggs in front of the fire.

"BUT are you still ALIVE???"
gasped the villagers.

"Indeed I AM!" said Esteban.
"As for the GHOST . . .
he is gone forever.
You will find his clothing scattered about the courtyard."

Esteban loaded his three bags of coins onto his donkey and rode off.
First he gave the *copper* coins to the poor.
Then he gave the *silver* coins to the church.
And on the *golden* coins
and the thousand golden rials from the castle's owner
he lived a life of luxury and ease
for many many years.

NOTES ON TELLING

Make the "Ooooohhh meeeee . . ." as penetrating and eerie as you can. I use
a high shrill tone that makes the little ones cover their ears and sends junior
high–age listeners into fits of giggles. I hold the call longer and gradually drop
it in tone on the last shriek, as the head falls down the chimney.

This tale seems to mesmerize any age. I remember in particular one eighth-grade class in Waianae, Hawaii, which pulled itself out of the stupor of a hot late-afternoon classroom and came to sudden life when I launched into this story. Just outside the school heavy construction trucks lumbered by noisily and it took effort on all of our parts to get beyond the heat, the torpor, and the racket, but I still remember the intensity of those listeners.

COMPARATIVE NOTES

This tale is H1411.1 *Fear test: staying in haunted house where corpse drops piecemeal down the chimney. Dead man's members call out to hero. "Shall we fall or shall we not?" Ghost laid by fearlessness. Rewarded with treasure.* In *Storyteller's Sourcebook* I cite variants from Spain (Ralph Steele Boggs, *Three Golden Oranges*, p. 99–108), Mallorca (Ruth Manning-Sanders, *Book of Ghosts*, p. 9–13), Wales (Elisabeth Sheppard-Jones, *Welsh Legendary Tales*, p. 167–172), and a variant use by Maria Leach in *The Thing at the Foot of the Bed* (p. 46–48). The telling given here is patterned after a tale by Ralph Steele Boggs and Mary Gould Davis, "The Tinker and the Ghost," in *Three Golden Oranges*. A picturebook version by Sibyl Hancock, with illustrations by Dirk Zimmer is titled *Esteban and the Ghost*. You may want to consult it for its amusing illustrations, but refer to Bogg's original rendition for the text.

The motif of a body that falls piecemeal down the chimney also appears as part of a series of scary episodes in several variants of H1440 *The learning of fear*. This is Type 326 *The Youth Who Wanted to Learn What Fear Is*, with variants listed as Finnish, Swedish, Estonian, Livonian, Lithuanian, Norwegian, Danish, Icelandic, Scottish, Irish, French, Spanish, Dutch, Flemish, German, Austrian, Italian, Sicilian, Rumanian, Serbo-Croatian, Slovenian, Polish, Russian, Greek, Turkish, Indian (Asian), Franco-American, English-American, Spanish-American, Chilean, Puerto Rican, Portuguese-American, West Indian, American Negro, Zuñi, and New Mexican. My *Storyteller's Sourcebook* lists children's versions of H1440 from Germany (Grimm's); Slovenia (Vladimir Kavčič, *The Golden Bird*, p. 50–70); and Portugal (Maurice and Pamela Michael, *Portuguese Fairy Tales*, p. 133–138).

Compare this tale with "The Strange Visitor" (page 133) in this collection. Though very different in tone, the motif of a body assembled from pieces is similar.

See *World Folktales* by Atelia Clarkson and Gilbert Cross and *The Thing at the Foot of the Bed* by Maria Leach for further notes on this tale.

THE CONJURE WIVES

Once upon a time,
when Halloween came on the dark of the moon,
there were three old conjure wives sittin' round the fire.
Cookin' supper for themselves.
Talkin' about the spells they was goin' to weave come midnight.

By and by there come a knockin' at the door.

> "Who's there?" called the old conjure wives.
> "Whooo? Whooo?"

A voice outside the door began to moan.
> "I'm cold and I'm hungry.
> Let me in dooo."

The old conjure wives all burst out laughin'.

"We's cookin' for ourselves.
Who'll cook for you?
Who? Who?"

"I'm cold through and through . . .
And I'm hungry tooo.
Let me in . . . doooo."

The old conjure wives just laughed.
"Get along. Do.
We's cookin' for ourselves.
Who'll cook for you?
Who? Who?"

Then the voice didn't say nothin'.
But the knockin' just kept on.

"Who's that knockin'?"
called the conjure wives.
"Who? Who?"

And the voice didn't say nothin'.
But the knockin' just kept on.

Then the old conjure wives went to work cookin' up their supper.

And the voice didn't say nothin'.
But the knockin' just kept on.

The old conjure wives hitched their chairs up to the fire.
And they ate and ate.

And the voice didn't say nothin'.
But the knockin' just kept on.

Then the old conjure wives called out again,
"Go away. Do!
We's cookin' for ourselves.
Who'll cook for you?
Who? Who?"

And the voice didn't say nothin'.
But the knockin' . . . just kept on.

Then those conjure wives began to get scared.
And one of them says,

"Let's give it somethin' and
get it away before it spoils our spells."

The old conjure wives took the littlest piece of dough they had.
A piece of dough about as big as a pea.
And they put that in the frying pan.

And the voice didn't say nothin'.
But the knockin' . . . just kept on.

And when that dough began to warm up in the frying pan . . .
it began to swell.
And that dough swelled and it swelled.
It swelled all over the frying pan and out onto the
   top of the stove.

And the voice didn't say nothin'.
But the knockin' . . . just kept on.

That dough just got bigger and bigger.
It covered the top of the stove and ran off onto the floor.

And the voice didn't say nothin'.
But the knockin' . . . just kept on.

The old conjure wives had to climb up onto the backs of their
   chairs.
The dough spread all over the floor and began to come up onto those
   chairs.

And the voice didn't say nothin'.
But the knockin' . . . just kept on.

Then those old conjure wives scrunched up on their chair backs.
They scrunched themselves smaller and smaller to get away from that
   awful rising dough.
And their backs hunched up . . . just like owls.
And their eyes got bigger and bigger with fright.
And they stared and stared . . . just like owls.

And they kept on callin',
        "Who's that knockin'?
        Who? Who?"

And the knockin' . . .
STOPPED.

And the voice called out,
>"I'm someone you should have been kinder to.
>Just keep on callin' 'Who . . . who . . . who . . . '
>It's the life of an owl in the woods for you!"

And those old conjure wives cackled and turned their
heads back and forth . . .
and they had beaks!
And they picked up their feet to get them out of that dough . . .
and they had claws!
And they tried to reach out their arms . . .
and they had wings!
And the dough just kept on risin' right up over the backs of their
    chairs.

And the voice called out,
>"Fly away! Do!
>There's no more house for You . . . You . . . You!"

Then all those old conjure wives could do was SPREAD their
    WINGS
    . . . and FLY out the window into the woods.
Callin' "Who'll cook for you?
Who? Who?"

And they're out there still.
Out in those dark woods.
Callin' their conjure-wife calls.
"Who'll cook for you?
Who? . . . Who? . . . "

You can go out and hear them if you don't believe me.

Only don't go out on Halloween night.

Cause that's when those old owls turn back into conjure wives . . .
a-sittin' and a-weavin' their spells.

NOTES ON TELLING

This story is really a mood piece. Its lack of explicit explanation bothers some
listeners. You might want to explain before you begin that conjure wives pos-
sess witchly powers, and that these conjure wives get turned into owls for their
stingy habits. We never learn just who the voice outside the door was, and this
seems confusing to some children. Whoever it was, it had stronger magic than
the conjure wives.

Let the audience knock with you when "the knockin' just kept on."
Three slow, heavy knocks work well. You must start the intensity of this piece
low, so you have room to build gradually to the climactic scene when the conjure wives SPREAD their wings and fly off.

COMPARATIVE NOTES

Frances G. Wickes included this story in her 1921 collection *Happy Holidays*.
It has been a favorite of library storytellers and is reprinted in Wilhelmina Harper, *Ghosts and Goblins* (p. 44–47); Elizabeth Hough Sechrist, *Heigh-Ho for
Halloween* (p. 9–12); Helen Hoke, *Spooks, Spooks, Spooks* (p. 157–160); and Virginia Haviland, *North American Legends* (p. 122–125). Wickes reported the tale
as a "Southern folktale" but did not cite her source.

The 1919 *Journal of American Folk-Lore* (v. 32, #125, p. 360) gives the
tale as "Digdee Owl." It includes only one woman and no swelling dough. Her
cry is "Whoo! Whoo! A whoo! Oh, you cook today and I cook to-morrow.
Whoo! Whoo! A who-o!" The 1891 *Journal of American Folk-Lore*, v. 4 (p.
171) contains a related chant. William H. Babcock's cook, a young black girl
from Fairfax County, Virginia, told him she heard this dialogue among owls.

He Owl: Who, who, who are you?

She Owl: Who, who, who are you?

He Owl: Who, who, who are you?

      Rough-shod, shoe-boot,

      Chicken soup so good,

      Who cooks for we-all?

She Owl: Who, who, who are you?

      I cooks for myself;

      Who cooks for yourself?

      Who cooks for we-all?

He Owl: Who, who, who are you?

She Owl: Who, who, who are you?

Chorus of Little Owls: Who, who, who are you?

This Southern tale must have evolved from the European tale A1958.0.1. *The owl is a baker's daughter who objected to the size of the dough put into oven for Jesus when he appeared in her house as a beggar.* She is turned into an owl for her stinginess. In *Storyteller's Sourcebook* I list variants from Britain and Norway for this tale. The Aarne-Thompson Type Index cites variants as Finnish, Swedish, Estonian, English, Italian, Czech, Slovenian, Russian, Turkish, Chinese, and English-American for Type 751A *The Peasant Woman Is Changed into a Woodpecker.* In some variants she is changed into a woodpecker or other bird instead of an owl. Baughman's *Type and Motif-Index of the Folktales of England and North America* cites sources for A1958.0.1 from England, Virginia (Negro), and North Carolina. He lists for Type 751A sources from the Isle of Skye, England, Virginia (Negro), Indiana, and Michigan (Negro). Baughman also notes Shakespeare's reference in *Hamlet,* "They say the owl was a baker's daughter." Katharine Briggs' *Dictionary of British Folktales* gives two variants of "The Owl Was a Baker's Daughter" (v. I, p. 124, p. 443). In the second of these it is a fairy disguised as a beggar woman who visits the baker's shop.

SOP DOLL

Once there was a boy named Jack.
Now Jack was BRAVE.
Haunts . . . or witches . . .
didn't scare Jack.

Heard about a mill over in the next county . . .
that was *haunted*.
Every boy that miller hired to stay in the mill
would be dead by morning.

Well Jack needed a job pretty bad.
Decided he'd hire on with that miller.
Miller says,

"Well Jack . . .
If you can get rid of whatever it is has got my mill
haunted . . .
I've got a bag full of gold here . . .
and I'll just *give* it to you."

Jack said, "Sounds good to me.
    But I'll need some food."

The miller brought him out a sack with a hambone in it . . .
had a little meat left on the bone.
Jack took that along . . .
went into the mill
and got set up for the night.

Now the mill was just one big room.
Had the grinding stones on one end . . . where the flour was
    ground.
Big water wheel outside to turn the mill stones.
Fireplace down at the other end of the room.
And all around the top of the room . . . up near the ceiling
were little tiny windows.
Twelve of them.

Well Jack built himself a big fire in the fireplace.
He took out his knife . . .
Jack had a real fine knife he'd got from his grandpap
And he always kept it honed *sharp*.
Jack cut some ham off his hambone
put it in his skillet
and commenced to fry it up.

Then he took out a bunch of candles he had . . .
twelve of them . . .
and set them all around him and lit them.

They lit the place up real well.
Jack didn't feel the least bit scared.
He grabbed up a handful of flour
threw it into his skillet along with the ham fryin's
and started makin' himself some gravy.

All of a sudden,
      "Whrrrr . . . Pssss . . . "

A black cat jumped up in one of them high windows.

      "I see I've got *company*," said Jack.

Then "Whrrr . . . Psss . . . "
Another black cat jumped up in the *next* window.
      "Whrrr . . . Pssss"
      "Whrrr . . . Pssss"
      "Whrrr . . . Pssss"

Cats began to appear at *all* of those windows.

      "Whrrr . . . Pssss . . . Whrrr . . . Pssss . . . Whrrr . . .
        Pssss . . .
      Whrrr . . . Pssss . . . Whrrr . . . Pssss . . . Whrrr . . .
        Pssss . . . "

And in the LAST window . . .
the biggest black cat of *all*.

"WHRRR . . . PSSSS. . . ."

And they all just sat and stared *down* at Jack

and twitched their long black tails.

Jack kinda poked his fire up a little brighter
and kept on stirrin' his gravy.

Pretty soon one of them black cats jumped down.
     "Rrrrr"

And walked up to where one of Jack's candles was burnin'.
Reached out its paw and . . . "pst!" . . . put it out.

Then another one jumped down . . .
     "Rrrrr"

Walked over . . .
stuck out its paw . . .
and . . . "pst!" . . .
put out another candle.

Down came another.
     "Rrrrr. . . . . pst!"
     "Rrrrr. . . . . pst!"
     "Rrrrr. . . . . pst!"

Those cats came jumping down there one after the other.
     "Rrrrr . . . pst! . . . Rrrrr . . . pst! . . . Rrrrr. . . . pst!

Rrrrr . . . pst! . . . Rrrrr . . . pst! . . . Rrrrr. . . .
pst! . . . "

Jack was left setting almost in the dark.
With those black cats sittin' all round him . . .
starin' . . .
and twitchin' their tails.

Then the biggest cat of all jumped down.
"RRRRR . . . . . . "

Reached out and put out that *last* candle.

"PST!"

Jack went on stirring his gravy.
But he watched mighty close to see what those cats
were going to try next.

That biggest cat sidled up to Jack . . .
kinda rubbed itself against his leg
like it was tryin' to get friendly.
Reached out and tried to stick its *paw* in Jack's *gravy*.
Cat says, "Sop *Dawlll* . . . "

Jack jerked his skillet back.
Says, "Don't you sop your *doll* in MY gravy."

Cat kinda purred around there for a minute.
Jack went back to stirrin' his gravy.
Cat stuck its paw out there again.

"Sop *Dawllll* . . . "

Jack jerked his skillet up.
      "You keep your *doll* out of my *gravy*!
      If you try to *sop your doll* in my gravy again
      I'll cut it OFF!"

Cat arched its back up
kinda squirmed around there
reached out its paw again
and STUCK IT RIGHT IN THAT GRAVY.

      "SOP DAWLLLL. . . .!"

Jack whipped out his knife.
Sliced that paw right off . . . clean as a whistle.

      "RRRRRRAAAAWWWWW!"

That black cat let out a YOWL. . . .
JUMPED out that window and disappeared.

      "RRRRAAAAWWWW!"
All the other cats followed.

Jack sat there.
Looked down at his frying pan.
There wasn't any CAT'S paw laying there . . .
it was a WOMAN'S HAND.
With a big *ring* on it.

      "Well," said Jack.

"I guess it was more than just CATS
come to visit me tonight."

Jack took his frying pan outdoors and scoured it real good.
Threw away that ham and gravy
'cause he guessed that old witch cat must have poisoned it.
And he was right.
That's how those old witches had been killing off the mill hands.
Stick their paws in the food and *poison* it.
Soon as the boys ate their supper . . .
they'd fall over dead.

Well when Jack had cleaned his skillet out good
he fried himself up some more ham and gravy.
Ate it.
And went to bed.

Next morning Jack put that witch hand in a gunny sack
and went to visit the Miller.
Said, "I'd like to see your wife, if I may."
Miller says, "Well my wife's upstairs in bed.
            Hurt her hand last night somehow."

Jack said, "Just let me talk to her alone for a minute."

Jack went in.
The Miller's wife was all scrunched up in bed with the covers pulled
    up.

        "Beg pardon, Mam," said Jack.
        "But I'd like to see your right hand."

She poked out her left hand.

"No Mam!
I'd like to see your RIGHT hand."

She kinda scrunched around
and poked out her *left* hand again.

Jack says, "I'm gonna have to have a look at your RIGHT hand." He
reached down and grabbed her right arm and pulled it out . . .
and there wasn't any HAND on it!

Jack says, "Well I guess we know what we *know*."

Says, "Now I'm gonna give you one chance.
You give me your cat skin.
And tell me the names of all those friends you was with last night.
And I'll burn those skins and we'll be rid of the witchin' in this
    neighborhood.
Or if you won't,
then I guess I'll just have to show your husband what's in this
    bag."

Well she pointed to her dresser drawer.
And Jack opened it
and there was that old black cat skin.
Tossed that in his gunny sack.

Went down the road and visited every one of her friends.
Collected all those black cat skins.
Went back to the mill
and had himself a big bonfire.

Burnt them all up.
And that was the end of the witching in *that* neighborhood.

Miller said, "I'm mighty grateful to you Jack.
	And here's that bag of *gold*
	just like I promised."

Jack took his gold and went along home.
And last time I heard
he was doin' right well.

NOTES ON TELLING

If you take your time, you can create quite effective imagery with sound effects as the cats leap up to their windows and hiss . . . one by one . . . "Whrrr . . . Pssss." You may want to create your own vocalizations for this. The image should be one of an alley cat leaping to a wall with a growl and hissing down at its victim. Repeat the effect as the cats leap down, growl, and reach out their paws to extinguish each candle. The "pst!" is the abbreviated sound of a candle being squenched.

COMPARATIVE NOTES

Motif G211.1.7 *Witch in form of cat* is a popular motif in British and U.S. folklore. Baughman's *Type and Motif Index of the Folktales of England and North America* lists 21 British and 26 American variants of this tale. Stith Thompson lists variants from Ireland, England, Wales, the U.S., Iceland, Switzerland, Germany, and Spain.

This particular tale, in which a witch in the form of a cat has her hand cut off, is Thompson motif D702.1.1 *Cat's paw cut off: woman's hand missing. A man spends a night in a haunted mill, where he cuts off a cat's paw. In the morning the miller's wife has lost her hand.* Thompson lists variants from England,

Ireland, the U.S., India, and Japan. Baughman gives three versions from the British Isles and U.S. variants from New England, New York, Maryland, Virginia, North Carolina, South Carolina, Georgia, Texas, Arkansas, Missouri, Kentucky, Indiana, and Illinois. He also cites variants from the Isle of Skye, Kentucky, and Indiana in which a hog's foot is cut off. In *Storyteller's Sourcebook* I cite children's editions of "Sop Doll" by Richard Chase (*The Jack Tales*, p. 76–82), Helen Hoke (*Spooks, Spooks, Spooks*, p. 141–146), and Maria Leach (*The Thing at the Foot of the Bed*, p. 96–98). I also cite a Japanese tale, "Old Woman Kowashi," in which a fish peddler attacked by cats beheads one.

This motif sometimes appears in conjunction with H1411.2 *Fear test: staying in haunted house infested by cats* (Type 326 *The Youth Who Wanted to Learn What Fear Is*). Also cited in *Storyteller's Sourcebook* is a Danish variant (Ruth Bryan Owen, *The Castle in the Silver Wood*, p. 41–48) as *H1411.2.0.1 *Hero whacks each of 13 cats as they leave, visits 13 sick women in morn and takes catskins.*

For my telling I drew on variants by Richard Chase (*The Jack Tales*, p. 76–82), Isobel Gordon Carter (*Journal of American Folklore*, XXXVIII, 1925, p. 353–354), and on *The Frank C. Brown Collection of North Carolina Folklore* (Vol. 1, p. 660–664).

For more discussion of this tale see notes in Maria Leach, *The Thing at the Foot of the Bed* (p. 122–123) and *World Folktales* by Atelia Clarkson and Gilbert Cross (p. 185–187).

Leach tells us that the word *doll* is an old Northumberland dialect word for a little child's hand, and *sop* means gravy. I prefer to think of *sop* as a verb . . . the cat is trying to *sop* its doll (paw) in the gravy. Chase says that his informant pronounced this phrase almost like "sop . . . darrr . . . "

You may want to compare this tale with "The Great Red Cat" (page 47) in this same collection. The tales begin similarly, with twelve black cats surrounding a lone man. But their plots then move in different directions.

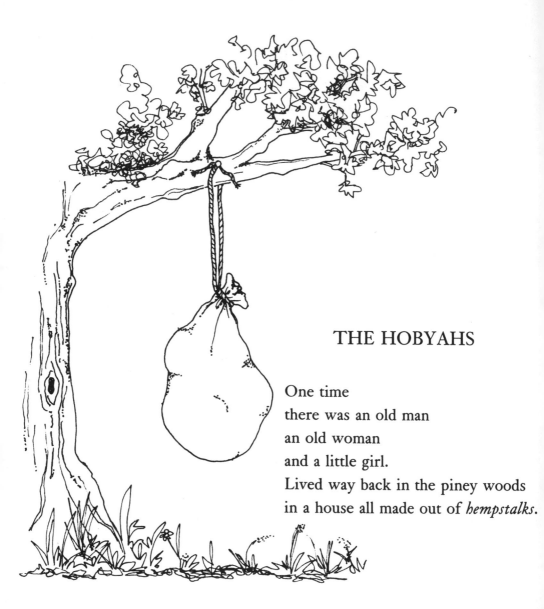

THE HOBYAHS

One time
there was an old man
an old woman
and a little girl.
Lived way back in the piney woods
in a house all made out of *hempstalks*.

They had a little dog
named LITTLE DOG TURPIE.

Now all around this house
in the deep dark piney woods
there lived lots and lots of HOBYAHS.

Hobyahs are fearsome beasts.
They come out of the woods at night
and gobble up little girls
and gobble up little boys
and they gobble up BIG FOLKS too.

One night
the Hobyahs came out of the woods.
They came dancing around the house and calling . . .

> "HOBYAH . . . HOBYAH . . . HOBYAH . . .
> TEAR DOWN THAT HOUSE OF HEMPSTALKS!
> GOBBLE UP THE OLD WOMAN . . .
> GOBBLE UP THE OLD MAN . . .
> AND CARRY OFF THAT LITTLE GIRL!"

But Little Dog Turpie . . .
he barked LOUD and LOUDER
and he frightened the HOBYAHS away.

Then woke the Old Man from his slumber.
> "Wife," says he,
> "I cannot sleep nor slumber.
> That Dog Turpie barks LOUD and LOUDER.
> And if I live till morning . . .
> I'm going to cut off his TAIL I am."

And in the morning . . .
do you know what that mean old man did?
He cut off Dog Turpie's tail.

That night the Hobyahs came again.
They came dancing around the house and hollering . . .

> "HOBYAH . . . HOBYAH . . . HOBYAH . . .
> TEAR DOWN THAT HOUSE OF HEMPSTALKS!
> GOBBLE UP THE OLD MAN . . .
> GOBBLE UP THE OLD WOMAN . . .
> CARRY OFF THAT LITTLE GIRL!"

But Little Dog Turpie barked LOUD and LOUDER
and frightened the HOBYAHS away.

Then woke the Old Man from his slumber.
> "Wife," says he,
> I cannot sleep nor slumber.
> That Dog Turpie barks LOUD and LOUDER
> and if I live till morning . . .
> I'm going to cut off his FRONT LEGS I am.

And in the morning . . .
you know what that mean old man did.
He cut off Dog Turpie's front legs.

That night the Hobyahs came again.
They came dancing around the house and calling fearfully.

> "HOBYAH . . . HOBYAH . . . HOBYAH . . .
> TEAR DOWN THAT HOUSE OF HEMPSTALKS.
> GOBBLE UP THE OLD MAN.
> GOBBLE UP THE OLD WOMAN.
> CARRY OFF THAT LITTLE GIRL."

But Little Dog Turpie barked LOUD and LOUDER
and he frightened the HOBYAHS away.

Then woke the Old Man from his slumber.
> "WIFE," says he,
> I cannot sleep nor slumber.
> That Dog Turpie barks LOUD and LOUDER.
> And if I live till morning . . .
> I'll cut off his HIND LEGS too I will."

And in the morning . . .
you know what that mean old man did . . .
He cut off Little Dog Turpie's hind legs.

That night the Hobyahs came again.
They came dancing around the house and calling fearfully . . .

> "HOBYAH . . . HOBYAH . . . HOBYAH . . .
> TEAR DOWN THAT HOUSE OF HEMPSTALKS.
> GOBBLE UP THE OLD MAN.
> GOBBLE UP THE OLD WOMAN.
> CARRY OFF THAT LITTLE GIRL."

Then woke the Old Man from his slumber.
> "WIFE," says he,
> I cannot sleep nor slumber.
> That Dog Turpie barks LOUD and LOUDER.
> And if I live till morning . . .
> I'll cut off his HEAD . . . I will."

And in the morning . . .

you know what that mean old man did . . .
He cut off Little Dog Turpie's head.

Poor Dog Turpie had no more tail,
no more legs,
and now he had no more head.

But that night the Hobyahs came again.
They came dancing around the house and calling FEARFULLY . . .

"HOBYAH . . . HOBYAH . . . HOBYAH . . .
TEAR DOWN THAT HOUSE OF HEMPSTALKS.
GOBBLE UP THE OLD MAN.
GOBBLE UP THE OLD WOMAN.
CARRY OFF THAT LITTLE GIRL."

Did Little Dog Turpie bark LOUD and LOUDER?
NO.
He COULD NOT.
He had no more head to bark with.

So the Hobyahs TORE down that house of hempstalks.
They GOBBLED up the old woman.
They GOBBLED up *that old man*.
And they carried off that Little Girl in a bag.

Deep, deep in the forest they took her.
And they tied the bag high in a tree.

All day long the Hobyahs slept.
And all night long

they'd DANCE around that tree . . .
take down the bag . . .
KNOCK on it . . .
open it and call,
        "LOOKA ME . . . LOOKA ME . . . LOOKA ME!"

tie the bag up . . .
and put it back in the tree again!

Little Girl cried and cried.
One day a Hunter came through the forest.
He heard the Little Girl crying.
He took DOWN the bag.
Took OUT the Little Girl.

And in the bag
he put his BIG HUNTING DOG!

That night the Hobyahs came home.
They DANCED around the tree . . .
took down the bag . . .
KNOCKED on it . . .
opened it and called,
        "LOOKA ME . . . LOOKA ME . . . LOOKA ME!"

And OUT jumped the big hunting dog
and gobbled them down . . .
every single one.

And so today
you and I need never be afraid
because there are NO MORE HOBYAHS.

*****

Well that's the way *I* heard the story.
But if you don't like leaving Little Dog Turpie in pieces,
I guess you can make up your own ending.
Something like . . .

> As for Little Dog Turpie . . .
> I've heard it said that he picked up the pieces . . .
> Pulled himself together . . .
> And ran off to Spain with the HUNTING DOG.

NOTES ON TELLING

Engage the audience in this tale by encouraging them to help with the doleful chant "Hobyah . . . Hobyah . . . Hobyah . . . " I like to pronounce this "Hoo-byah" and direct it as a tongue-in-cheek eerie call. It is really quite ludicrous and junior high and teen listeners will love mocking the Hobyah's absurd call. Everyone usually has a good time with this silly tale. But it is probably not best to tell the tale to younger audiences containing serious dog lovers. Keep the tone of the piece as light as possible and watch to see that no one is turning green during your telling.

Several authors and tellers have changed the ending to soften the tale. I feel that the tale might as well be told as is, or not at all. But I have added a softer ending here so that the child reader may select the ending preferred.

The tale's collector, S. V. Proudfit, noted in 1891 that "the effectiveness of the story lies in a certain sepulchral monotone in rendering the cry of the Hobyah, and his terrible 'look me.'"

On repeated tellings of this story the audience becomes involved in the rhythm and the word play and seems less concerned about the plot. They love to provide Dog Turpie's bark on the line "That Dog Turpie barked LOUD and LOUDER," and of course they say the entire Hobyah chant with you. I find it best to provide the audience with a small entrée into participation on the first telling and let their level of participation increase on repeated tellings.

When I speak of repeated tellings, I think particularly of the classroom teacher, who will be asked to repeat a story several times if the children like it.

COMPARATIVE NOTES

The origin of this tale is sketchy. It appeared in the 1891 *Journal of American Folklore*, contributed by S. V. Proudfit of Washington, D.C. "When a child, I used to hear the following story told in a Scotts family that came from the vicinity of Perth. Whether the story came with the family I am unable to say," says Proudfit.

The story was reprinted by Joseph Jacobs in *More English Fairy Tales* (p. 127–133) with only minor alterations, and has become a favorite of library storytellers despite its gory plot. The tale appears in Phyllis Fenner's *Giants, Witches, and a Dragon or Two* (p. 174–177) and in Virginia Tashjian's *Juba This and Juba That* (p. 51–54).

The story has been softened by some storytellers. Carolyn Sherwin Bailey (*Stories Children Want*, p. 6–10) leaves the little girl out of the story entirely and has the little old woman carried away. The old man "takes off his tail," then relents and gives Dog Turpie back his parts. Dog Turpie tracks down the Hobyahs, cuts the bag open, and rescues the little old woman. Leila Berg (*Folk Tales for Reading and Telling*, p. 64–70) gives a version based on Bailey.

Simon Stern's picture book, *The Hobyahs*, retells the story with a happy ending also. He shows them all living happily together in a turnip house.

The tale includes motifs G441 *Ogre carries victim in bag*, and K525.6 *Escape, leaving dog as substitute*. In *Storyteller's Sourcebook* I classify the tale under B332.1* *Too watchful dog killed*. Baughman classifies this as a cumulative tale, Z21.5*, because of the piecemeal cutting up of the dog on consecutive nights.

OLD BEN

This is a mighty pitiful story.
All about Old Ben
my Unc Spiv's favorite coon dog.

Now my Unc Spiv was quite a coon hunter when he was a boy.
One night Unc Spiv and his Grandpop were sittin' by the fire with
   their boots off . . .
Gettin' about ready to go to bed . . .
When the hound dogs began to bark.
And then Old Ben . . .
He began to bark too.

      "Grandpop," says Unc Spiv.
      "If you don't care too hard
      why don't we go out and have us a coon hunt?"

Grandpop didn't care too hard.
So they put on their boots.
Got their shotgouns
Went out and turned those hound dogs loose.
Then Old Ben
they turned him loose too.

Those hound dogs tore up the South holler
a-barkin' coon.
And Old Ben tore up the South holler
barkin' coon too.

Then those hound dogs tore over that hill
a-barkin' coon.
And Old Ben tore over that hill
a-barkin' coon too.

Those hound dogs tore down that East holler
a-barkin' coon.
And Old Ben tore down that East holler
a-barkin' coon too.

Then they treed.
And those hound dogs all commenced a-barkin' tree.
And then Old Ben chimed in . . .
and he treed too.
And Grandpop says, "We got him!"

Caught up with them dogs and Unc Spiv says to Grandpop,
        "Grandpop if you don't mind too hard

I think
I'll climb up in that tree and knock that old coon down.
And we'll have ourselves a dog and coon fight."

Grandpop didn't care too hard.
So Unc Spiv climbed up that tree.
Just about got out to where he could knock that coon off of the limb
when that coon gave a LEAP
and jumped right on Unc Spiv's BACK!

Unc Spiv fell out of that tree
right into the middle of that pack of hound dogs
with that coon right on top of him.
All those dogs piled on there
with Unc Spiv under it all.

"Grandpop,
if you don't mind too hard
you might pull a few of these hound dogs off of me,"
says Unc Spiv.

Grandpop started swinging at those dogs with his lantern
and By Gollies, he broke that lantern.

There they were in the dark.
Grandpop tryin' to pull off hound dogs,
Unc Spiv tryin' to get out from under,
the hound dogs tryin' to bite coon,
and the coon tryin' to bite dog.

After a while Grandpop got all the dogs pulled off.

So Unc Spiv felt around and got hold of that coon and hefted it up.
And it was the biggest old coon he'd ever hefted.

Says "Grandpop,
If you don't care too hard
I think I'll skin this old coon right here
and just carry home the skin."

Grandpop, he didn't care too hard.
So Unc Spiv whipped out his skinnin' knife and skinned that old
    coon.
Rolled up the skin
and they went along home.

Grandpop called the hound dogs
and they all come.
Then he called Old Ben
and reckon he come too.

Got along home.
And I'm sad to tell you
this is the end of the story.
'Cause
got in the house
rolled that old skin out on the floor . . .
and By Gum, they'd skinned Old Ben.

NOTES ON TELLING

This story is usually told in the first person, as if it happened to the teller (usually a man). To make it work for me, I retold it as if the story had happened to my uncle. To tell the truth, this tale is a little too terrible for my own taste. But the fifth grade boys on whom I tested this material insisted that "Old Ben" go in the book.

COMPARATIVE NOTES

I based this story on "An Arkansas Folk Tale—'Old Ben'" by August Rubrecht (*Southern Folklore Quarterly*, 1966, December, v. XXXX #4, p. 342–343). Rubrecht says he collected the tale in 1960 from John Tillman, a native of Benton County, Arkansas. He notes that it had often been told in Bayless Community and around Pea Ridge, Arkansas.

I recall hearing the story told in a coffeehouse in San Francisco in 1962. The tale is still current among professional storytellers.

I use "Spiv" Helt's name in the story because it reminds me so much of a true story he tells. When he was a boy they had a coon that they kept as a house pet. One night they heard the dogs begin to bark and Spiv and his brothers all ran out with their shotguns. They shot three coons out of one tree! And the first one they shot out . . . was their own pet coon. There is a lot of pathos in that story the way Spiv tells it, and it reminded me of "Old Ben."

SAM'L

There was a fellow named Samuel.
Called *Sam'l*, he was.

Poor Sam'l was killed in a fire.
House burnt down
and Sam'l with it.

When the fire burnt out
Sam'l picked himself up
shook himself
and discovered . . .
he was a GHOST.

Started walking about the world.

And now he was *dead* . . .
he saw all manner of creepy, ghostly things around him.
Bogles . . . and slimy things . . . all about.
Sam'l didn't like it at all.

And the bogles and ghosties all leered at Sam'l and said,
"You must go to the Great Worm in the graveyard
and be eaten.
You'll never be able to rest till that's done.
Go Sam'l . . .
Go and be EATEN."

So Sam'l went to the graveyard.
And there was a great slimy worm . . . all coiled round.
And the thing uncoiled itself when it saw Sam'l coming.
It stuck its great ugly head right into Sam'l's face
and said,
"Ooohhh . . . it's Sam'l come to be eaten is it?"

Sam'l shook all over.
But he knew it had to be done.
He covered his head with his hands
and waited.
"*EAT ME.*"

The Great Worm snuffled all around Sam'l.
Snuffled around . . .
and snuffled around . . .

"I can't eat thee Sam'l.
There's no *body* here.
Where's your body?"

"Oh, it was burnt in the fire I reckon," says Sam'l.

"Well go back and fetch the ashes.
And then we'll see," said the Worm.

So Sam'l went back to the place of the fire.
And he collected all the ashes.
Brought them back to the Graveyard Worm.

"Here's the ashes.
I reckon they're all there," said Sam'l.

And he began to tremble.

"Now . . .
EAT ME."

The great horrid Worm stuck out its ugly head
and snuffled around . . .
and snuffled around . . .
and turned the ashes all over . . . snuffling.

"SAM'L! There's still some'at missing," said the Worm.
"There's an *arm* gone here."

"Oh that," said Sam'l.
"I had an arm cut off in an accident one time."

"Well I can't eat thee without it's all here," said the Worm.
"Go and fetch the arm."

So Sam'l went out
and searched and searched
and finally he found that arm
where it had been buried.
So he took the arm back to the Great Worm.

"Here's the arm.
And here's the ashes," said Sam'l.

And he was shivering with fright.
"Now *EAT ME*."

The Great Worm stuck out its huge, ugly head.
It snuffled around . . .
and snuffled around . . .

"SAM'L! There's still some'at missing here.
I make it your *right thumbnail* is missing yet."

"Oh, well yes. I did lose a thumbnail.
And it never growed back."

"Sorry Sam'l.
I can't eat thee without everything is here.
You'd best go look for that thumbnail."

So Sam'l went back to look.

Now finding an arm is one thing . . .
but a thumbnail?
Sam'l looked and looked . . .

He never *did* find that thumbnail.
He's looking still I hear.

Sometimes he'll see a thumbnail before him . . .
"That's IT!" he'll think.
And *grab* for it.
Then find it's fastened onto someone else's hand.

So if you ever feel something tugging away at your thumbnail . . .
speak real quick and say,
> "No Sam'l! No!
> It's not thine.
> Go look somewhere else!"

And Sam'l will go away.

NOTES ON TELLING

I discovered this story while looking for some really terrible tales for this book. I assume that just as some readers will find my own Halloween favorites, such as "The Hobyahs," too horrid for telling, other readers will like material which is too horrid for *my* taste . . . which this tale frankly is. I have told it for just one Halloween season as of this writing, and found myself dropping the tale from my program whenever the audience looked a bit impressionable. But the fifth and sixth grade boys at Lynn Black's Community School (Kirkland, Washington) insist that "Sam'l" go into the book. And it does fit my criteria . . . it's a good story and quite terrible!

If you are fond of dialects you may want to consult the lovely language in the Katharine Briggs text (*see* Comparative Notes for citation). I have tried to keep the flavor of her text, which had already been anglicized from the heavy dialect of the original, but have simplified some of the more awkward phrases.

COMPARATIVE NOTES

This tale is taken from "Sammle's Ghost" in Katharine M. Briggs, *A Dictionary of British Folk-Tales*, Part B, Vol. 1, p. 563–564. Briggs takes the tale from M. C. Balfour, "Legends of the Cars," in *Folk-Lore* II, p. 415. She has anglicized the text to make it more readable. She cites this tale as E419.7 *Person with missing bodily member cannot rest in grave*, and suggests that it explains the belief behind motif E235.4 *Return from the dead to punish theft of part of corpse*. The tale seems also to be related to E752.5 *Lost soul gnawed by worms*, which has several Irish variants cited by Tom Peete Cross in his *Motif-Index of Early Irish Literature* (Bloomington, Indiana, 1952). D415.2 *Man eaten by worm as punishment* seems related, as does B99.2 *Mythical worm.*

I have been unable to locate more information on the mythology of this incredibly vivid character . . . the graveyard worm. The term "worm" in British folklore often refers to a serpent or dragon, but here the "worm" must be just that . . . an enlarged maggot. Anyone who has seen maggots at work in rotting flesh should have no trouble with the imagery intended. This mythic beast seems to survive today only in the children's song . . . "the worms crawl in . . . the worms crawl out . . . the worms play pinochle on your snout. . . ."

A similarly horrid tale, "The Flying Childer," is retold in Alan Garner's *Book of British Fairy Tales* (p. 141–145). This is based on a tale collected by Mrs. Balfour in "Legends of the Cars," *Folk-Lore, II*, p. 403–409. Katharine Briggs reprints it in her *Dictionary* of *British Folk-Tales, Part B, Folk Legends, Vol. 1*, p. 453–454. In this gruesome tale of chopped-up corpses begging for burial, a murdered murderer flees to the graveyard and *begs* a great worm to eat him. The worm has the head of the girl he has murdered and it takes its time in eating him though he implores it to be quick.

I have made one slight motif change in this tale. The tugging on thumbnail motif at the end is my own invention. It seemed quite logical, since Sam'l is wandering still. Briggs' text concludes " . . . if he's not found his nail, he's walking about seeking for it." Then the informant added, "That's all. Granfer told me one day when I were asking where all the bogles come from. 'Tis not much of a tale, but I can't mind another now, and it's sort of funny, isn't it?"

THE CAT WITH THE BECKONING PAW

This is the story of a cat so loyal it was willing to give its life for its mistress.

A Japanese lady had a pet cat that never left her side.
This cat followed her about and watched over her at all times.

One day a swordsman, a samurai, came to call on the lady.
As they sat talking,
the lady's cat suddenly began to yowl.
It leaped onto the lady and began to bite and claw at her kimono.
The lady jumped up.
But the cat continued to leap at her,
shredding her silk kimono and yowling.

The samurai, thinking the cat had gone mad,

drew his sword and . . .
beheaded the leaping cat.

The cat's body fell into a corner of the room.
But its head . . . flew into the air and fastened its teeth on a
    poisonous serpent hanging from the rafters . . .
just over the head of the lady.

The cat had been trying to warn its mistress of this terrible
    danger.
Even in its death the cat's head managed to fix its teeth on the viper
and save the life of its mistress.

That cat's devotion is remembered to this day.
The lady had a statue made in the image of her cat.
She kept this statue in a place of honor in her room.

Today a statue of this cat is found in
many Japanese stores sitting by the cash register,
a symbol of good fortune and prosperity.
The cat is always shown with its paw raised
as if beckoning the passerby to come nearer.

This tiny cat who saved its mistress is known throughout Japan.

NOTES ON TELLING

Small statues of the lucky cat are available for under five dollars in most Japanese novelty shops. If you can acquire one to show, it will make the story more meaningful. There is a woodcut depicting the "beckoning cat" in Pratt and Kula's *Magic Animals of Japan* which could be shown.

COMPARATIVE NOTES

A brief version of this story appears in Davis Pratt and Elsa Kula, *Magic Animals of Japan* (Parnassus, 1967). The couple heard the stories in their collection while living in Japan. Ikeda (Hiroko Ikeda, *A Type and Motif-Index of Japanese Folk-Literature*) and Thompson give Japanese variants of the tale under B524. 1.3 *Cat kills attacking rat*. A most interesting discussion of the tale appears in Dr. M. W. de Visser's "The Dog and the Cat in Japanese Superstition," *Transactions of the Asiatic Society of Japan*, v. 37, 1909–1910 (p. 23–25). De Visser cites several variants of that tale in which the pet is a dog who saves its master. A temple is built to honor the sacrificing dog. In one tale the dog was considered a messenger of the Bodhisattva. In another, the tale was placed in the Tensho era (1573–1591) and Utsu Tadashige, the Lord of Kamiwada and Shimowada, was said to have killed his white dog in anger as it tried to warn him of a snake in a tree above. The dog's head jumped up and killed the snake. The Lord buried the dog's head and tail at Kamiwada and Shimowada and erected the Shinto temples known as the temples of the "Dog's head and tail" in those places. The *Kwagetsu Soshi*, written by Matsudaira Sadanobu (1757–1829), tells the tale of a girl saved by her pet cat. My research does not make it clear just how the dog temple story became attached to the lucky cat figurine.

TOTANGUAK

Many Eskimo children are expert at string figures. There is even a string figure spirit, named Totanguak, who lurks outside at night hoping to find some child who will wake up and play with him. If you play string figure games with Totanguak and he wins, the spirit will take you away with him forever.

There once was an Eskimo boy who lived with his father in
   an igloo.
One evening when his father was asleep the boy woke up.
He didn't want to go back to sleep.
Instead, he took out his string and began to play string figures.

First he made the figure of the polar bear.
Then he made the figure of the Northern Star.
Then he made his favorite figure . . . the falling down tent.

As the boy made the tent
he told himself the story of how a snowstorm came suddenly
and broke down the tent.
The two little boys inside ran away in opposite directions.
All this was acted out in the string figure.

The little boy was having a fine time playing string figures.
Suddenly he felt as if there were someone else inside the igloo.
He looked around . . .
there by the entrance a man was sitting.

> "Hello," said the man.
> "I see you like to play string figures.
> Could I play with you?"

The little boy was pleased to have someone to play with.
> "See . . . I have my own string," said the man.

He pulled out his long string.

> "Let's have a contest and see who can make string figures
> the fastest."

> "All right," said the little boy.

This boy knew many string figures and could make them very
rapidly.

> "I'll name the first figure we shall make," said the man.

> "Go ahead."

> "The figure we will make is. . . . *The Polar Bear*."

The little boy knew this one.
He began quickly to weave the string on his fingers.
But already the man had finished!

"You are good at this!" said the little boy.

"Oh . . . I know a string figure or two," said the man.

"Well it's *my* turn to name the string figure we shall make
     next," said the little boy.
"Let's make . . . *The Falling Down Tent.*"

The little boy knew this figure very well.
He made the tent, dropped the strings,
and the little boys ran away.
He won!

"Well . . . you are very good too," said the man.
"Why don't we play two out of three . . . for winners."

"All right."

The little boy was sure he could win.

"But don't forget it's *my* turn to name the figure we will
     make this time," said the man.

"That's fair."

The little boy got ready to begin the string figure.

He knew many string figures.
What would the man name . . . ?

      "The string figure we shall make . . . ," said the man,
      "is the string figure called . . .
      TOTANGUAK!"

The little boy shrank in horror.

He knew now that he was playing with the string figure spirit
   himself . . .
TOTANGUAK!

If he didn't win this game,
Totanguak would take him away forever.

And the string figure called Totanguak is so complicated
that it takes yards and yards of string to complete.

But the boy had to *try*.

He began weaving the first steps of the figure on his hands . . .
Then he looked up.

Totanguak had already used all of the string on his hands
and he had begun to TAKE OUT HIS OWN INTESTINES . . .
and weave them into the figure . . .
yard . . . after yard . . . after yard . . .
until he held one great glistening mass
woven into the string figure called
TOTANGUAK.

The little boy knew he had lost.
He knew he would be taken away forever.

But just then his father woke up and sat up in bed.
Totanguak vanished.
The little boy was saved.

Never again did he take out his string to play
when he should have been sleeping.

And let this be a lesson to you.
If you cannot sleep at night
don't get up and begin to play games.

Just turn over and go back to sleep,
lest you should look over in the corner of your room
and see . . .
TOTANGUAK . . .
waiting to play with *you*.

NOTES ON TELLING

Tell your audience about the Eskimo spirit Totanguak before you begin the story, explaining that he will carry away any child who plays string figure games with him and loses.

Use your string as a prop as you tell this story, pretending to pull it out of your pocket as Totanguak pulls out his string, beginning to weave a figure as the little boy tries to compete, and completing the Falling Down Tent as the boy makes it. This is the only figure you have to learn for telling the story.

1. Place your string behind the thumb and little finger and in front of the three middle fingers of each hand. Hold the hands apart and check to make sure this matches the illustration.

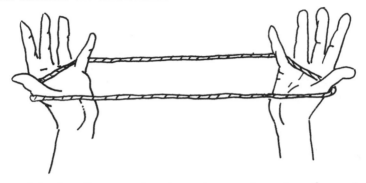

2. Put your right forefinger under the string on the palm of your left hand.

3. Picking up the string on the back of the forefinger, pull it back until your hands are in a spread-apart position again.

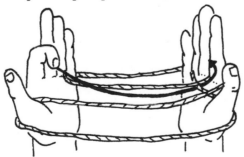

4. Repeat with the left forefinger, picking up the palm string from the right hand. (You are now in what is often called "Position A" in books on the making of string figures.)

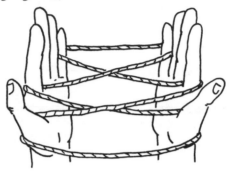

5. Curl the four fingers of each hand forward and close them against the heel of your thumb, trapping all of the strings in your palms securely, but leaving free the string nearest you which passes around the outsides of the two thumbs.

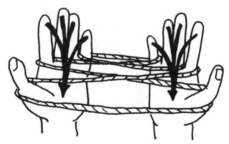

6. Now flip your hands over so that this thumb string flops over to the backside of your hands. It is now running around the backs of your hands and crossing below your little fingers.

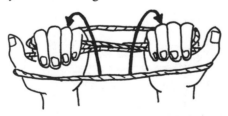

7. With your thumbs reach through, over the low front string riding on the crotch of your thumbs, and clear to that lowest string in the back. Pick that back low string up on the backs of your two thumbs and pull it forward into your hands-stretched-apart position.

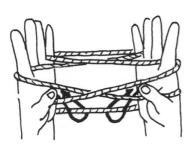 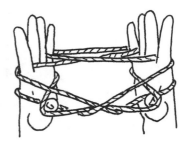

8. Now comes the tricky part. Without dropping any strings, reach over the left hand, pick up the string lying on the back of the left hand, pull it over the left hand and drop it in the palm of the left hand. Now do the same thing for the right hand back-of-hand string, dropping it in the palm of the right hand.

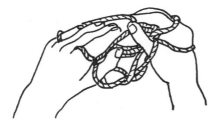

9. Spread your hands apart, pointing your fingers at your audience, and show them the tent figure you have created.

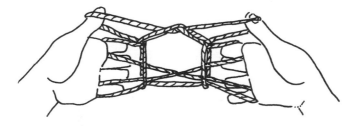

125

10. Shake the figure to simulate the snowstorm breaking the house down, then reach forward with your right hand and remove the string loop from your left forefinger, dropping it into your left palm. Do the same for your right forefinger loop.

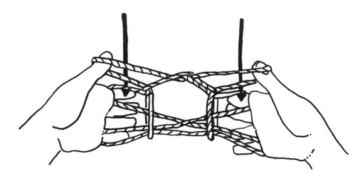

11. Spread your hands apart dramatically and pull. Two loops should travel out the strings toward each palm. This is the two little boys running away from the collapsed tent.

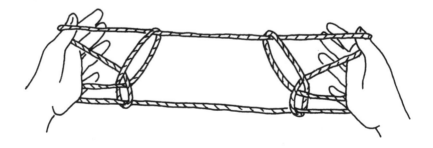

You should make the figure twice, once while the little boy is playing alone at the tale's beginning, acting out the figure as the story directs, and once again during the contest. I take quite a bit of time with the string figure during the first use, showing it around to make sure the entire audience can see the little boys run off. I sometimes repeat it so everyone gets a chance to watch. The second time it must be done as rapidly as possible, as you are in the heat of the contest.

When Totanguak begins pulling out his own intestines . . . yard . . . after yard . . . after yard . . . you should glory in this. Demonstrate and hold the "great glistening mass" up in your own hands. This is delightfully grue-some. Play to your audience and "gross them out." Adults are disgusted . . . kids love it. For audiences under grade three, explain what intestines are before you begin.

COMPARATIVE NOTES

The story of "Totanguak, Spirit of String Figures" is included in Edward Field's *Eskimo Songs and Stories* (collected by Knud Rasmussen on the Fifth Thule Expedition, illustrated by Kiakshuk and Pudlo, New York: Delacorte Press/Seymour Lawrence, 1973, p. 38–41). Field cites his source as "the offi-cial records of Rasmussen's voyages published by the Royal Danish Archives."

A similar tale is told by A. L. Kroeber in his article "Tales of the Smith Sound Eskimo," *Journal of American Folklore*, v. XII, 1899 (p. 166). A boy play-ing at seal knuckle-bones while the old people sleep is called out to play by a TuTuaTuin. His father warns him to wear his father's boots and trousers and his mother's jacket. Thus the TuTuaTuin cannot take him.

Harry and Elizabeth Helfman discuss Eskimo string figures in their *Strings on Your Fingers*, but they do not give us a source for their information. Of the spirit of the strings they write: "A crackling sound in the hut meant that this unseen spirit had arrived. Those inside the hut were breathless with fear. Quickly they raised their hands with the string around them, and again and again, faster and faster, made the same figure the spirit was making with its in-visible string. The trick was to beat the spirit at his own game; then he would go away" (p. 9–10).

In telling this story I have incorporated an eskimo string figure, "A Siberian House and Two Eskimos Running Away," from the Helfmans' book (p. 22–23). The string figure is also given in *String Figures and How to Make Them: A Study of Cat's Cradle in Many Lands* by Caroline Furness Jayne (Dover, 1962, p. 361). This was originally published by Scribner's in 1906 as *String Figures*.

THE RED SILK HANDKERCHIEF

This English story was recounted by a Devonshire farmer who knew the girl to whom this had happened.

There was a young girl named Joanna
who fell in love with a handsome young man.
When they were engaged to be married
he gave her a red silk handkerchief as a token of their love.
Before the marriage could take place, however,
the young man died.

After some time had passed
Joanna agreed to marry a farmer in the neighborhood.

The night after she had made her pledge to this farmer
she was awakened by a tapping on the stairs in her house.

A hoarse voice seemed to whisper,
"Joanna Joanna return to me
the red silk handkerchief
I gave to thee."

"It's only a rustling on the stairs," she thought.
But she took the red silk handkerchief from her chest
and held it in her hand.

Then there came a tapping on her door.

"Who's that tapping on my door?"

"Joanna Joanna return to me
the red silk handkerchief
I gave to thee."

"Perhaps it is only the wind," she thought.
But she put her head under the covers.

Next there came a tapping on the foot of her bed.

"Who's that tapping on my bed?"

"Joanna Joanna return to me
the red silk handkerchief
I gave to thee."

"That's more than the wind," she thought.
And when she heard something sliding up over the footboard

she threw back the covers
tossed the red silk handkerchief at the apparition
and screamed,

"Take it!
Take it!
Leave me be!"

The ghost vanished
and the red silk handkerchief with it.

Friends said she had dreamed all this.
But the red silk handkerchief was never seen again.

Joanna swears that if you were to open her lover's coffin
you would find that same red silk handkerchief
clutched to his breast.

NOTES ON TELLING

You might try hiding a red silk scarf on your person and flinging it into the
audience on the line "Take it!"

COMPARATIVE NOTES

This tale is retold from Katharine M. Briggs' *A Dictionary of British Folk-Tales*,
Part B, Vol. 1 (p. 560). She reprints it from S. Baring-Gould's *A Book of
Folk-Lore*; the tale must have been collected in the late 1800's.

The tale is Thompson Motif E211 *Dead sweetheart haunts faithless
lover*. Many similar tales are found in Thompson motifs E200–E299, all of

which deal with "Malevolent return from the dead." In *Storyteller's Sourcebook* I list several similar tales from children's collections including the familiar "Golden Arm" (E235.4.1), "Teeny-tiny" (E235.4.3), "Chunk O' Meat" (E235. 4.3.1*), and "Tailypo" (E235.4.3.2*). Our heroine in this tale is treated fairly well by her lover's ghost; often the dead lover carries his sweetheart off back to the grave with him as in Type 365 *The Dead Rider (Lenore)*.

THE STRANGE VISITOR

There was an old woman
sat all alone in her cabin one night
spinning her wool.

And so she sat . . .
and so she spun . . .
and so she waited
for someone to come.

Then . . .

there came a *knocking* at the door.

"Come in!" called the old woman.

"Screeeak . . . " went the door.

And in came a pair of BIG BIG FEET.
Sat themselves down
on the COLD COLD FLOOR.

> "How STRANGE," said the old woman,
> " . . . to see such BIG BIG FEET
> on this COLD COLD FLOOR."

But . . .
Still she sat . . .
and still she spun . . .
and still she waited
for someone to come.

Then . . .
> "KNOCK. KNOCK. KNOCK."

> "Come in!" called the old woman.

> "Screeeak . . . " went the door.

And in came a pair of SHORT SHORT LEGS.
Sat themselves down
on the BIG BIG FEET
on the COLD COLD FLOOR.

> "How STRANGE," said the old woman,
> " . . . to see such SHORT SHORT LEGS
> on those BIG BIG FEET
> on this COLD COLD FLOOR."

But . . .
Still she sat . . .
and still she spun . . .
and still she waited
for someone to come.

Then . . .
        "KNOCK. KNOCK. KNOCK."

        "Come in!" called the old woman.

        "Screeeak . . . " went the door.

And in came a WEE WEE WAIST.
Sat itself down on the SHORT SHORT LEGS
on the BIG BIG FEET
on that COLD COLD FLOOR.

        "How STRANGE," said the old woman,
        " . . . to see such a WEE WEE WAIST,
        on those SHORT SHORT LEGS
        on those BIG BIG FEET
        on this COLD COLD FLOOR."

But . . .
Still she sat . . .
and still she spun . . .
and still she waited
for someone to come.

Then . . .

"KNOCK. KNOCK. KNOCK."

"Come in!" called the old woman.

"Screeeak . . . " went the door.

And in came a pair of BROAD BROAD SHOULDERS.
Sat themselves down
on the WEE WEE WAIST
on the SHORT SHORT LEGS
on the BIG BIG FEET
on the COLD COLD FLOOR.

"How STRANGE," said the old woman,
" . . . to see such BROAD BROAD SHOULDERS
on that WEE WEE WAIST
on those SHORT SHORT LEGS
on those BIG BIG FEET
on this COLD COLD FLOOR."

But . . .
Still she sat
and still she spun
and still she waited
for someone to come.

Then . . .
"KNOCK. KNOCK. KNOCK."

Come in!" called the old woman.

"Screeeak . . . " went the door.

And in came a pair of LONG LONG ARMS.
Sat themselves down
on the BROAD BROAD SHOULDERS
on the WEE WEE WAIST
on the SHORT SHORT LEGS
on the BIG BIG FEET
on the COLD COLD FLOOR.

"How STRANGE," said the old woman,
" . . . to see such LONG LONG arms
on those BROAD BROAD SHOULDERS
on that WEE WEE WAIST
on those SHORT SHORT LEGS
on those BIG BIG FEET
on this COLD COLD FLOOR."

But . . .
Still she sat
and still she spun
and still she waited
for someone to come.

Then . . .
"KNOCK. KNOCK. KNOCK."

"Come in!" called the old woman.

"Screeeak . . . " went the door.

And in came a pair of LARGE LARGE HANDS.

137

Sat themselves down
on the LONG LONG ARMS
on the BROAD BROAD SHOULDERS
on the WEE WEE WAIST
on the SHORT SHORT LEGS
on the BIG BIG FEET
on that COLD COLD FLOOR.

"How STRANGE," said the old woman,
" . . . to see such LARGE LARGE HANDS
on those LONG LONG ARMS
on those BROAD BROAD SHOULDERS
on that WEE WEE WAIST
on those SHORT SHORT LEGS
on those BIG BIG FEET
on this COLD COLD FLOOR."

But . . .
Still she sat
and still she spun
and still she waited
for someone to come.

Then . . .
"KNOCK. KNOCK. KNOCK."

"Come in!" called the old woman.

"Screeeak . . . " went the door.

And in rolled a BIG BIG HEAD!!!

Sat itself down
on those BROAD BROAD SHOULDERS
with the LARGE LARGE HANDS
on the LONG LONG ARMS
and the WEE WEE WAIST
on the SHORT SHORT LEGS
on the BIG BIG FEET
on that COLD COLD FLOOR.

"OOOOOHHHH . . . ," said the old woman.
"Where did you get such BIG BIG FEET?"

"MUCH WALKING.
MUCH WALKING."

"Where did you get such SHORT SHORT LEGS?"

"MUCH RUNNING.
MUCH RUNNING."

"Where did you get such a WEE WEE WAIST?"

"MUCH BENDING.
MUCH BENDING."

"Where did you get such BROAD BROAD
    SHOULDERS?"

"SWINGING AN AXE.
SWINGING AN AXE."

"Where did you get such LONG LONG ARMS?"

"THRESHING WHEAT.
THRESHING WHEAT."

"Where did you get such LARGE LARGE HANDS?"

"CARRYING *BROOMSTICKS.*
CARRYING *BROOMSTICKS.*"

"Where did you get such a . . .
BIG BIG HEAD?"

"It's a PUMPKINSHELL!
It's a PUMPKINSHELL!"

"What did you come to *my* house for . . . ?"

"TO GET YOU!!!"

NOTES ON TELLING

This works well as audience participation. Let the audience knock with you, call "Come in," and then "screeeak" the door. They may also like to join on the "How strange" refrain. And all will want to rock, spin, and chant with you on the "Still she sat . . ." lines. Some tellers use a hand motion on the spinning line which involves the hands circling each other, palms toward the body, rather like winding a ball of yarn.

The story is often told to preschool and primary grade children as a flannel board story. It is quite a silly story when told that way, as the cut-out body parts are thought very amusing. Patterns are found in Judy Sierra's *The Flannel Board Storytelling Book* and in Paul Anderson's *Storytelling with the Flannel Board*, but I suggest you design your own pumpkinhead.

Be sure to consult Jacobs' version before learning this story. You may prefer to learn the more exotic language of his original and use the strange wail "*Aih-h-h!*—late—and *wee-e-e* moul" which his creature gives. I use that version when telling this to older groups, but have given the clearer version that I use for preschoolers here. The use of a pumpkinhead for the creature is a matter of taste. It is not in the original, but it works well.

COMPARATIVE NOTES

I learned this story from two Alameda County children's librarians who presented it with a flannel board at a California workshop in 1969. I scribbled down the tale outline and began telling it immediately. Later I discovered several printed sources for the tale.

A favorite of teachers and librarians, this tale appeared in R. Chambers' *Popular Rhymes of Scotland* (Edinburgh, 1890, p. 64), and was included in Joseph Jacobs' *English Folk and Fairy Tales*, first published in 1890. The story must have pleased storytellers of the time, for by 1926 it had already been anthologized in at least five collections, according to listings in Mary Huse Eastman's *Index to Fairy Tales, Myths, and Legends*. Those editions are out of print now, but my *Storyteller's Sourcebook* lists three contemporary versions in addition to Jacobs' (which is still in print): Walter De La Mare, *Animal Stories* (p. 386–388); Elizabeth Hough Sechrist, *Heigh Ho for Halloween* (p. 48–51); and Amabel Williams-Ellis, *Fairy Tales of the British Isles* (p. 132–134).

Paul S. Anderson's version in *Storytelling with the Flannel Board* uses a "pumpkinshell head" motif. Chambers' original replies that the head is so large because of "muckle wit." And in Chambers' version the creature replies to questions about "Where did you get such small small legs?" with a wail "*Aih-h-h!*—late—and *wee-e-e* moul." He answers half of the questions and replies with this wail to the other half. Some tellers find this very effective. See Jacobs' text for his anglicized version of Chambers.

Katharine Briggs includes the Chambers version in her *A Dictionary of British Folk-Tales*, Part A. Folk Narratives, Vol. 2, p. 560–561. She suggests that the reassembled skeleton is Death personified and that the wailing chorus is reminiscent of keening. See both Briggs and Jacobs for further notes.

In *Storyteller's Sourcebook* I cite this tale under Z13.1 *Tale teller frightens listener: yells "boo" at exciting point.* The tale also is related to H1411.1 *Fear test: staying in haunted house where corpse drops piecemeal down the chimney.* See "The Tinker and the Ghost" (page 69) in this collection for notes on that tale.

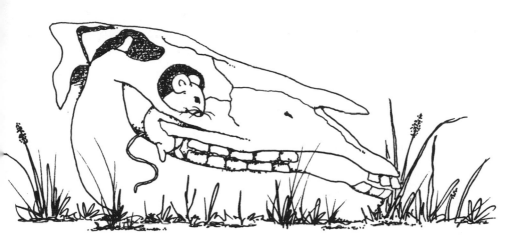

WHO LIVES IN THE SKULL?

A horse's skull lay in a field.
It had been bleached white by the sun and rain.

Little-Mouse-Creep-Along came along and saw the skull.

> "What a fine house for me!
> It's a white bone palace for a little mouse!"

And he moved right in and set up housekeeping.

The next day along came
Frog-Croak-a-Lot.

> "Who lives in the skull?
> Who lives in the skull?"

"It's me. Little-Mouse-Creep-Along.
Who are you?"

"I'm Frog-Croak-a-Lot.
May I come into your house?"

"If there's room for me
there's room for you!
You can come in too."

So Frog-Croak-a-Lot came into the skull.

The next day up hopped
Hare-Hide-in-the-Hill.

"Who lives in the skull?
Who lives in the skull?"

"It's Little-Mouse-Creep-Along
and Frog-Croak-a-Lot.
Who are you?"

"I'm Hare-Hide-in-the-Hill.
May I come into your house?"

"If there's room for us
there's room for you!
You can come in too."

So Hare-Hide-in-the-Hill came into the skull.

The next day along came
Fox-Run-Everywhere and Wolf-Leap-out-of-the-Bushes.

"Who lives in the skull?
Who lives in the skull?"

"Little-Mouse-Creep-Along,
Frog-Croak-a-Lot,
and Hare-Hide-in-the-Hill.
Who are you?"

"It's Fox-Run-Everywhere and Wolf-Leap-out-of-the-
Bushes.
May we come into your house?"

"If there's room for us
there's room for you!
You can come in too!"

So Fox-Run-Everywhere and Wolf-Leap-out-of-the-Bushes
came into the skull.

By this time the skull was very crowded.
The animals were pushing and shoving and talking.
But everyone was having a grand time.
"The more the merrier" they thought.

Then along came Bear-Squash-the-Whole-Lot-of-Them.

"Who lives in the skull?
Who lives in the skull?"

145

"Little-Mouse-Creep-Around,
Frog-Croak-a-Lot,
Hare-Hide-in-the-Hill,
Fox-Run-Everywhere,
and Wolf-Leap-out-of-the-Bushes.
Who are you?"

"I'm Bear-Squash-the-Whole-Lot-of-Them.
May I come into your house?"

"If there's room for us
there's room for you!
You can come in too!"

So Bear-Squash-the-Whole-Lot-of-Them
walked right up . . .
sat himself down on the horse's skull . . .
and SQUASHED-THE-WHOLE-LOT-OF-THEM!

NOTES ON TELLING

As you tell, make a skull of one hand. Join thumb and forefinger to form the "eye" and curl other fingers around as skull. Move the fingers of the other hand into the skull through the "eye" one by one as they call out their names and enter. I use my thumb for Mouse, index finger for Frog, etc. I wiggle the questioning finger as it "talks," then tuck it into the skull. Since I can't wiggle the last two fingers independently of each other, my Fox and Wolf approach *together*. When Bear arrives remove the "skull" hand and close the other into a tight fist to represent the skull and inhabitants. Let the former "skull" hand now become Bear. Lower it and SQUASH-THE-WHOLE-LOT-OF-THEM!

If this were done with a single child on your lap your hands could be the bear and squash the child's hands. If I am working with a small group of preschoolers whom I know well, I sometimes tell the story this way and run around squashing all of their hands.

COMPARATIVE NOTES

Another variant of this story shows the animals entering a lost mitten until it breaks apart. In my *Storyteller's Sourcebook* the mitten tale is classed as J2199.5* *Fools (usually animals) invite all comers to join them in abode until house ruptures.* Alvin Tresselt's *The Mitten* uses this motif, as does the paperback *The Mitten: A Ukrainian Fairy-Tale* (Moscow, 1979). I classify the skull tale as J2199.5.1* *Animals invite all comers to join them living in horse's skull* and cites two Russian sources for the tale, Arthur Ransome's *Old Peter's Russian Tales* (p. 228–230) and James Riordan's *Tales from Central Russia* (p. 76–77). A variant titled "The Castle of the Fly" is found in Aleksandr Afanas'ev's *Russian Fairy Tales* (p. 25–26). In the Afanas'ev version, "A fly built a castle, a tall and mighty castle." This changes the theme of the tale to one of foolish pride by small animals, rather than the foolishness of not foreseeing an obvious outcome which characterizes the other variants.

A related tale is found in Bonnie Carey's *Baba Yaga's Geese*. In her tale "A Forest Mansion," fly, mosquito, wasp, and horsefly enter a basket. Spider spins them all in while they argue about who should go out first (MacDonald L396).

Note also the similarity of this tale to Sorche Nic Leodhas' Scottish rhyme *Always Room for One More*, in which a house fills with invited guests until it bursts. The tale is also reminiscent of the Nigerian tale "Why the Sun and Moon Live in the Sky" (MacDonald A736.1.4.4*), best known in Elphinstone Dayrell's picturebook version. Water is invited to visit and bring in more and more of his people, until Sun and Moon are forced to leave their house.

LET'S GO ON A GHOST HUNT!

LEADER:

Want to go on a Ghost Hunt?
Then repeat everything I say
and do everything I do.

                                             AUDIENCE:

All right?	All right!
Let's go!	Let's go!

(Begin to walk in place while slapping thighs with hands.
Keep this up during the following chant.)

Oh look!	Oh look!

148

There's a bridge!	There's a bridge!
Can't go 'round it.	Can't go 'round it.
Can't go under it.	Can't go under it.
Better go *over* it.	Better go *over* it.
All right.	All right.
Let's GO.	Let's GO.

(Beat your chest to make thumping noises for crossing the bridge. When you reach the other side, begin walking again.)

Oh look!	Oh look!
There's a field!	There's a field!
Can't go 'round it.	Can't go 'round it.
Can't go under it.	Can't go under it.
Better go *through* it.	Better go *through* it.

(Make motions of parting grass and tiptoeing through, making "swishhh . . . swishhh" sounds. After you've crossed the field, begin walking again.)

Oh look!	Oh look!
There's a swamp!	There's a swamp!

Can't go 'round it.   Can't go 'round it.

Can't go under it.   Can't go under it.

Better wade *in* it.   Better wade *in* it.

(Pretend your hands are boots: pick them up one by one and make
sucking noises with your mouth as you wade across the swamp.
When you reach the other side, start walking again.)

Oh look!   Oh look!

There's a stream!   There's a stream!

Can't go 'round it.   Can't go 'round it.

Can't go under it.   Can't go under it.

Better swim *through* it.   Better swim *through* it.

All right.   All right.

Let's GO.   Let's GO.

(Make swimming motions with your arms; after you've crossed the
river, begin walking again.)

Oh look!   Oh look!

There's a tree!   There's a tree!

Can't go 'round it.   Can't go 'round it.

Can't go under it.	Can't go under it.
Better go up it.	Better go up it.
Have a look around.	Have a look around.

(Make motions of climbing tree. When you reach the top, put hand to brow and look out one way.)

Oooooohhhhhhh . . .	Oooooohhhhhhh . . .

(Look out the other way.)

Ooooohhhhhhh . . .	Ooooohhhhhhh . . .
I see a house.	I see a house.
It looks like a haunted house.	It looks like a haunted house.
Let's go.	Let's go.

(Climb back down tree and begin walking again.)

Oh look!	Oh look!
There's the house.	There's the house.
I think it *is* haunted.	I think it *is* haunted.
Can't go under it.	Can't go under it.
Can't go over it.	Can't go over it.

Better go IN it.

Better go IN it.

All right.

All right.

Let's go.

Let's go.

(Walk very softly and
cautiously as you enter the Haunted House.)

OOOOOOHHHHHHH!

OOOOOOHHHHHHH!

It's DARK in here!

It's DARK in here!

I see some stairs.

I see some stairs.

Better go up them.

Better go up them.

(Walk upstairs cautiously.)

I see a dark, dark door.

I see a dark, dark door.

Better *open* it.

Better *open* it.

(Open door with one hand, making screeching noise.)

Oh NO!

Oh NO!

(Reach out your hand as if feeling something.)

I *feel* something.

I *feel* something.

It feels like a GHOST.

It feels like a GHOST.

(Put your hand to your ear.)

I *hear* something   I *hear* something.

(Make an eerie sound.)

It *sounds* like a GHOST.   It *sounds* like a GHOST.

(Cup hands around your eyes and peer ahead.)

I *see* something.   I *see* something.

It *looks* like a GHOST.   It *looks* like a GHOST.

IT *IS* A GHOST!!!!!   IT *IS* A GHOST!!!!

(Jump into air.)

LET'S GET OUT OF HERE!   LET'S GET OUT OF HERE!

(Retrace your steps as rapidly as possible, making all the motions.)

Out the door . . .
Down the steps . . .
Out of the haunted house . . .
Up the tree . . .
Down the tree . . .
Across the stream . . .
Through the swamp . . .

Across the field . . .
Over the bridge . . .
Back home and
SLAM THE DOOR!

NOTES ON TELLING

You may "walk" through this story by either marching in place, slapping your thighs rhythmically, or both. Keep the pace slow and steady on the way to the haunted house. Speak the lines of the chant right in time to your slapped legs. On the way back, make all of the motions as rapidly as possible but be sure everyone has gotten up the tree before you start back down again. You will arrive home EXHAUSTED.

COMPARATIVE NOTES

This tale is usually told as "Let's go on a Bear Hunt" with a bear in a cave as the ending scare. It is one of those well known bits of folklore that everyone knows but which seldom gets put into print. My version was learned during a sorority rush party at Indiana University in the fall of 1960. I have never heard a version quite like this one. Like the true folk game that this is, it seems to have a variant for each teller. A version called "The Lion Hunt" appears in print in Virginia A. Tashjian's *Juba This and Juba That: Story Hour Stretches for Large or Small Groups*, p. 62–70. A picture book version by Illinois children's librarian Sandra Stroner Sivulich (*I'm Going on a Bear Hunt*, illustrated by Glen Rounds, New York: E. P. Dutton, 1973) contains her version of the bear hunt.

THE TALE OF A BLACK CAT

Draw as you tell the story.

Once there was a little boy named Tommy.
Here's a T and that stands for "Tommy."
Tommy had a girlfriend named Sally.
Here's an S . . . that stands for "Sally."

One day Tommy decided to build himself a new house.

So he made a wall here . . .
and a wall here . . .
and a floor here . . .
What *else* does his house need?

That's right . . . a window . . .
I'll put a window in this room . . .
and a window in this room . . .

Let's put a door here . . .
and a door here . . .
and I'll make a doorstep here . . .
I think I'll plant some grass
    by the doorstep to make it look pretty.

What else do I need? . . .
A *chimney* . . . that's good.
I'll put a chimney on
    for this room . . .
and one for this room . . .

Tommy *liked* his new house.
    He said, "I think I'll go over to Sally's and tell *her*
    about my new house!"

So Tommy went over to Sally's house.
    Said, "Sally,
      why don't you come over
        and see the new *house*
    I just built?"

Sally said, "All right.
    But let's go down in the basement
      and get some apples to eat on
    the way over."

They went down in the basement at
    Sally's house
got some apples
and came out the basement door.

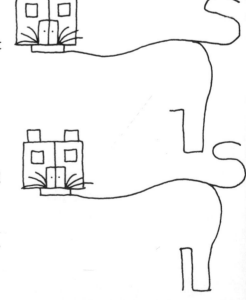

They just went two steps
and they fell down in a mud puddle!

Climbed out of that puddle,
went along over to Tommy's house.

They got almost there
and they fell down in a mud puddle
    again!

Climbed out of that puddle . . .
just went two steps . . .
and they fell down in a *mud puddle*
   again.

Climbed out of that puddle
and went along up to Tommy's
   house . . .
got almost there and Sally *stopped.*

Sally said,
        "I'm *not* going to go
           in that house!"

Tommy said,
        "Why not?"

        "'Cause I'm afraid of that
         BIG BLACK CAT!!!"

NOTES ON TELLING

Draw with chalk on a blackboard, or use a wide black felt tip pen on poster paper. Anne Pellowski suggests covering the cat's head with one hand while drawing the rest of the body, but I simply warn precocious classes, "If you've heard this one before . . . don't tell." This keeps someone from blurting out "It's a CAT!" before I am finished. Surprisingly, most children do not see the cat until you name it. Of course, once you have been doing drawing stories with a class, they try to guess ahead of you.

Involve the audience by asking them what to draw onto Tommy's house. They will call out several ideas; select those you planned to use anyway—"That's right . . . he needs a *door*."

Let the children make their own drawings after you finish, or let them take turns telling and drawing for the class. Drawing with white chalk on black construction paper will make handsome pictures to decorate your room at Halloween (thanks to Peggy Hart of Marysville, Washington, for this idea).

COMPARATIVE NOTES

Anne Pellowski includes a variant of this tale in *The Story Vine* (New York: Collier MacMillan, 1984, p. 48–51). She discusses the tale and cites several sources: Ida C. Craddock, "The Black Cat" in *Journal of American Folklore*, v. X, 1897 (p. 322–323); Charles Lutwidge Dodgson "Mr. T. and Mr. C." in *The Diaries of Lewis Carroll*, edited by Roger Lancelyn Green, Vol. 2, Appendix (New York: Oxford University Press, 1954); and Maud G. Early, "The Tale of the Wild Cat," *Journal of American Folklore*, v. X, 1897 (p. 80).

The story has been published in picturebook format by Carl Withers (*The Tale of a Black Cat*, illustrated by Alan Cober, New York: Holt, Rinehart, and Winston, 1966) and in a variation by Paul Zelinsky (*The Maid and the Mouse and the Odd-Shaped House* (New York: Dodd, Mead, 1981). Zelinsky's version is based on the 1897 notebook of a Connecticut schoolteacher. The tale also appeared in Clifton Johnson, *The Oak-Tree Fairy Book* (Boston, 1905). An even earlier version appeared in James Orchard Halliwell-Phillipps' *Popular Rhymes and Nursery Tales* (London: John Russell Smith, 1949). The "Game of the Cat" is listed under "Slate Games, " p. 114–116.

WITCHES' BREW

This must be told using an overhead projector. Place a shallow, transparent dish on the glass surface of the overhead. A glass pie plate or casserole works fine. Arrange your audience facing the wall where you project your "stew." They will have their backs to you and will see the ingredients only as they appear projected from the overhead. Ask the audience to repeat everything you say. Begin by teaching this chant and having them repeat it over and over while you stir the stew.

WITCHES' BREW . . .
WITCHES' BREW . . .
WITCHES STIR THEIR GHASTLY STEW . . .

WITCHES' BREW . . .
WITCHES' BREW . . .
WITCHES STIR THEIR GHASTLY STEW . . .

(When you are ready, begin adding the ingredients,
naming them as you drop them into the water)

BILE OF FROG . . .   (squirt of green cake coloring)

AND BONE OF BAT . . .   (cardboard bat bone)

LIZARD'S TAIL . . .   (crinkled piece of yarn)

AND EYE OF CAT . . .   (large drop of cooking oil)

WITCHES' BREW . . .   (all chant while you stir)
WITCHES' BREW . . .
WITCHES STIR THEIR *GHASTLY* STEW . . .

SLIME OF SLUG . . .   (squirt of green cake coloring)
AND TOE OF COOT . . .   (cardboard cutout)
BLOOD OF MORTAL . . .   (drops of red cake coloring)
EYE OF NEWT . . .   (small drops of cooking oil)

WITCHES' BREW . . .
WITCHES' BREW . . .
WITCHES' STIR THEIR *GHASTLY STEW* . . .

WEB OF SPIDER . . .   (tangled thread)
GALL OF CAT . . .   (yellow cake coloring)
POISON VENOM . . .   (blue cake coloring)
TOOTH OF RAT . . .   (small, sharp pointed stone)

WITCHES' BREW . . .

WITCHES' BREW . . .
WITCHES STIR THEIR GHASTLY STEW.

ADD THE DARK AND DEADLY DUST . . .
AND THE SPELL IS FINISHED . . . THUS!!!

(Dash in a generous glug of Bromo
Seltzer crystals; the stew will fizz and turn black!)

NOTES ON TELLING

This "stew" is a surefire hit, and makes a nice conclusion to a Halloween story-time. Be sure you have your ingredients hidden from your audience so they can't see what you are really putting in the stew. The fizzing Bromo Seltzer and suddenly darkened screen make a dramatic finish. Dash it in and stir frantically as you gasp, "And the spell is finished . . . THUS!!!"

COMPARATIVE NOTES

There is a whole genre of "teacher lore" afoot these days. A clever idea appears in a teacher's magazine, or is invented by a classroom teacher. The idea strikes everyone's fancy and soon the entire school is using it, then the district. Teacher's networks are far-reaching, and it doesn't take long for the idea dreamed up by a classroom teacher in Squim, Washington, to reach the classroom teacher in Tallahassee, Florida. This "Witches' Brew" is an example of such lore. I learned it in the spring of 1979 from Eva Holen, my daughter's second-grade teacher. Eva had a lengthy typed out story about a witch which she read as she put in the ingredients. It had been given to her by a teacher from another school, was nicely typed up and mimeographed, but cited no source. I wasn't interested in the wordy, somewhat forced story, but I was intrigued by the use of the overhead. Children's Librarian Marian Taylor and I were team-telling at Halloween that year, and we put together the chant I've given here.

Part II: Sources

SHORT SPOOKY TALES

These short tales may be read aloud or told.

"The Bogles from the Howff" from *Heather and Broom* by Sorche Nic Leodhas (p. 113–128). New York: Holt, Rinehart & Winston, 1960.

"Blood on His Forehead" from *Ghosts and Spirits from Many Lands* by Freya Littledale (p. 135–138). Garden City, N.J.: Doubleday, 1970.

"Bucca Dhu and Bucca Gwidden" from *Peter and the Piskies* by Ruth Manning-Sanders (p. 98–102). New York: Roy, 1958.

"The Buried Moon" from *More English Fairy Tales* by Joseph Jacobs (p. 102–108). New York: Putnam, 1894.

"Chunk o' Meat" from *Grandfather Tales* by Richard Chase (p. 231–233). Boston: Houghton Mifflin, 1948.

"The Goblins at the Bath House" from *Book of Ghosts and Goblins* by Ruth Manning-Sanders (p. 14–20). New York: Dutton, 1968, 1969.

"The Golden Arm" from *English Folk and Fairy Tales* by Joseph Jacobs (p. 143–144). New York: Putnam, n.d.

"Knurre-Murre" from *Animal Stories* by Walter De La Mare (p. 71–73). New York: Scribner's, 1939, 1940. (Also in *Book of Dwarfs* by Ruth Manning-Sanders, p. 49–53. New York: Dutton, 1963, 1964.)

"The Leg of Gold" from *Book of Ghosts and Goblins* by Ruth Manning-Sanders (p. 124–127). New York: Dutton, 1968, 1969.

"Mr. Fox" from *English Folk and Fairy Tales* by Joseph Jacobs (p. 153–158). New York: Putnam, n.d. (Also in *Twenty Tellable Tales* by Margaret Read MacDonald, p. 154–162. New York: H. W. Wilson, 1986)

"Old Gally Mander" from *American Folk and Fairy Tales* by Rachel Field (p. 295–302). New York: Scribner's, 1929.

"Old One Eye" from *Grandfather Tales* by Richard Chase (p. 205–214). Boston: Houghton Mifflin, 1948. (Also in *Twenty Tellable Tales* by Margaret Read MacDonald, p. 43–51. New York: H. W. Wilson, 1986)

"The Old Witch" from *More English Folk and Fairy Tales* by Joseph Jacobs (p. 101–106). New York: Putnam, 1894.

"The Old Woman and the Bear" from *With a Wig With a Wag* by Jean Cothran (p. 55–57). New York: McKay, 1954.

"The Ring" from *Book of Ghosts and Goblins* by Ruth Manning-Sanders (p. 87–89). New York: Dutton, 1968, 1969.

"The Sprightly Tailor" from *Celtic Folk and Fairy Tales* by Joseph Jacobs (p. 68–71). New York: Putnam, n.d.

"The Tailor in the Church" from *Book of Ghosts and Goblins* by Ruth Manning-Sanders (p. 43–46). New York: Dutton, 1968, 1969.

"Wait Till Martin Comes" from *Ghosts and Goblins* by Wilhelmina Harper (p. 195–198). New York: Dutton, 1936.

"The Witches' Ride" from *Ghosts and Goblins* by Wilhelmina Harper, (p. 228–233). New York: Dutton, 1936.

See also these entire collections:

Leach, Maria. *The Thing at the Foot of the Bed and Other Scary Tales*. Cleveland: World, 1959.

———. *Whistle in the Graveyard: Folktales to Chill Your Bones*. New York: Viking Press, 1974.

Mendonza, George. *Gwot: Horribly Funny Hairticklers*. New York: Harper & Row, 1967.

Schwartz, Alvin. *Scary Stories to Tell in the Dark*. New York: J. B. Lippincott, 1981.

TELLABLE FOLKTALES
IN PICTURE-BOOK FORMAT

The pictures may help you learn the tale. Read the book aloud a few times, then try telling the tale without consulting it. Make the picture book available for browsing after storytime.

Bang, Betsy. *The Old Woman and the Red Pumpkin: A Bengali Folktale*. Trans. and adapted by Betsy Bang. Illustrated by Molly Garrett Bang. New York: Macmillan, 1975.

Bennett, Jill. *Teeny Tiny*. Illustrated by Tomie de Paola. New York: Putnam's, 1986.

Galdone, Joanna. *The Tailypo: A Ghost Story*. Illustrated by Paul Galdone. New York: Seabury, 1977.

Galdone, Paul. *King of the Cats*. Illustrated by author. New York: Houghton Mifflin/Clarion, 1980.

———. *The Teeny Tiny Woman: A Ghost Story*. Illustrated by author. New York: Clarion, 1984.

Seuling, Barbara. *The Teeny Tiny Woman*. Illustrated by author. New York: Viking, 1976.

Young, Ed. *The Terrible Nung Guama*. Adapted from Leslie Bonnet. Illustrated by Molly Garrett Bang. New York: Macmillan, 1975.

ENHANCE YOUR STORYTIME WITH POETRY

Many Halloween story collections include poetry selections, and a bit of searching should turn up a few that will fit your own style. My favorite scary poetry collection is Jack Prelutsky's *Nightmares*. Children writhe with delight at these poems. Best of all is "The Bogeyman," with "The Ghoul" and "The Vampire" not far behind. And for a very effective counterpoint at midstory-time, pass out rhythm sticks and let the group clatter along with you as you read "The Dance of the Thirteen Skeletons." All clack rhythmically on the chorus: "And they'll dance in their bones. . . ." A flick of your hand should tell them when to clatter away and when to fall silent.

Prelutsky, Jack. *The Headless Horseman Rides Tonight: More Poems to Trouble Your Sleep.* Illustrated by Arnold Lobel. New York: Greenwillow, 1980.

———. *Nightmares: Poems to Trouble Your Sleep.* Illustrated by Arnold Lobel. New York: Greenwillow, 1976.

BELIEF LEGENDS

The kind of terrifying story that children tell each other at slumber parties and around campfires is of a different genre than the stories we usually tell at school and library storytimes. When kids ask for a really scary story, they hope to hear a tale of supernatural events that actually occurred. These tales are usually said to have happened to "a friend of a friend." They are believed to be true by the teller, or at least are not totally disbelieved. One such tale is "The Vanishing Hitchhiker," told about a hitchhiker who is picked up on a remote road one dark night, converses for a while, and then mysteriously vanishes. On inquiry the strange rider is found to match the description of a person killed on the same spot years earlier.

It is difficult to draw an exact line at the point where a "belief legend" loses its potency, is no longer believed, and becomes a less powerful "folktale." Stories in this collection such as "The Tinker and the Ghost" and "The Great Red Cat" probably were once told as true stories. They are far enough removed from contemporary notions of the supernatural for us now to hear them as simple folktales. The format in which they are told also marks them as "folktales," rather than "belief legends." A "believed" story begins "You know, a funny thing happened to my Aunt Lucy when she was down in Kentucky last year . . . ," not "On a dark and stormy night. . . . "

You may want to use caution in your telling of "belief legends" in storytimes because this material can be powerful and frightening. Much of its effect depends on how it is told, and whether you yourself believe the legends to be true.

Here is a brief bibliography to help acquaint you with the genre.

Brunvand, Jan Harold. *The Choking Doberman and Other "New" Urban Legends.* New York: W. W. Norton, 1984.

———. *The Vanishing Hitchhiker: American Urban Legends and Their Meanings.* New York: W. W. Norton, 1981.

Stories circulating in the U.S. recently. These are usually believed to be true by the teller. Many of Brunvand's "urban legends" deal with horrid happenings—spider's nests in beehive hairdos, murdered babysitters—but several tales of the supernatural are also included, such as the stories of the vanishing hitchhiker and the gangster ghost in the cadillac.

Degh, Linda. "The 'Belief Legend' in Modern Society: Form, Function, and Relationships to Other Genres." *American Folk Legend: A Symposium*, ed. Wayland D. Hand (Berkeley: University of California Press, 1971), p. 55–68.

Technical article defining the genre.

McNeil, W. K. *Ghost Stories from the American South*. Little Rock: August House, 1985.

Ghost legends believed by some to be true.

BIBLIOGRAPHY OF WORKS CONSULTED

Aarne, Antti, and Stith Thompson. *The Types of the Folktale*. Folklore Fellows Communications, No. 184. Helsinki: Suomalainen Tiedeakatemia, 1973.

Afanas'ev, Aleksandr. *Russian Fairy Tales*. New York: Pantheon, 1945, 1973.

Anderson, Paul. *Storytelling with the Flannel Board*. Book 1. Minneapolis: T. S. Denison, 1970.

Asbjørnsen, Peter Christen, and Jørgen Moe. *Norwegian Folk Tales*. New York: Viking, 1960.

Babcock, William H. "Folk-Lore Jottings from Rockhaven, D.C." in "Notes and Queries." *Journal of American Folk-Lore*, Vol. IV, Jan.–March 1891, p. 171.

Bailey, Carolyn Sherwin. *Stories Children Want*. Milton Bradley, 1931.

Baughman, Ernest W. *Type and Motif-Index of the Folktales of England and North America*. Indiana University Folklore Series, No. 20. The Hague: Mouton & Co., 1966.

Berg, Leila. *Folk Tales for Reading and Telling*. Cleveland: World, 1966.

Bettelheim, Bruno. *The Uses of Enchantment: The Meaning and Importance of Fairy Tales*. New York: Knopf, 1976.

Boggs, Ralph Steele, and Mary Gould Davis. *Three Golden Oranges and Other Spanish Folk Tales*. Illustrated by Emma Brock. New York: McKay, 1936, 1964.

Briggs, Katharine M. *A Dictionary of British Folk-Tales*. Bloomington: Indiana University Press, 1970.

Brown, Frank C. *The Frank C. Brown Collection of North Carolina Folklore*. 7 vols. Durham, N.C.: Duke University Press, 1952–64.

Carey, Bonnie. *Baba Yaga's Geese and Other Russian Stories*. Illustrated by Guy Fleming. Bloomington: Indiana University Press, 1973.

Carter, Isobel Gordon. "Mountain White Folk-Lore: Tales from the Southern

Blue Ridge." *The Journal of American Folklore*, Vol. XXXVIII, No. 144, 1925, p. 353–354.

Chambers, Robert, compiler. *Popular Rhymes of Scotland*. Edinburgh: W. and R. Chambers, 1890.

Chase, Richard. *The Jack Tales*. Illustrated by Berkeley Williams. Boston: Houghton Mifflin, 1943.

Clarkson, Atelia, and Gilbert B. Cross. *World Folktales: A Scribner Resource Collection*. New York: Scribner's, 1980.

Colwell, Eileen. *Round About and Long Ago: Tales from the English Countryside*. Illustrated by Anthony Colbert. Boston: Houghton Mifflin, 1972.

Craddock, Ida C. *The Black Cat.*" *The Journal of American Folklore*, Vol. X, 1897, p. 322–323.

Cross, Tom Peete. *Motif-Index of early Irish Literature*. Bloomington: Indiana University Press, 1952.

De La Mare, Walter. *Animal Stories*. New York: Scribner's, 1939, 1940.

de Visser, Dr. M. W. "The Dog and the Cat in Japanese Superstition." *Transactions of the Asiatic Society of Japan*, Vol. 37, 1909–10, p. 23–25.

Degh, Linda. "The Living Dead and the Living Legend in the Eyes of Bloomington Schoolchildren." *Indiana Folklore and Oral History*, Vol. 15, No. 2, 1986, p. 127–152.

Early, Maud G. "The Tale of the Wild Cat." *The Journal of American Folklore*, Vol. X, 1897, p. 80.

Eastman, Mary Huse. *Index to Fairy Tales, Myths and Legends*. 2nd ed. Boston: F. W. Faxon, 1926.

Eby, Cecil D., Jr., and Jack B. Moore. "The Wizard Clip: An Old Potomac Legend." *The Southern Folklore Quarterly*, XXV, No. 4, 1961, p. 256–260.

Fenner, Phyllis. *Giants, Witches, and a Dragon or Two*. Illustrated by Henry C. Pitz. New York: Knopf, 1943.

Field, Edward. *Eskimo Songs and Stories*. Collected by Knud Rasmusen on the Fifth Thule Expedition. Illustrated by Kiakshuk and Pudlo. New York: Delacorte Press/Seymour Lawrence, 1973.

Filmore, Parker. *Shepherd's Nosegay: Stories from Finland and Czechoslovakia.* Illustrated by Enrico Arno. New York: Harcourt, Brace & World, 1919, 1958.

Gastner, Theodor H. *The Oldest Stories in the World.* Boston: Beacon, 1952.

Hancock, Sibyl. *Esteban and the Ghost.* Illustrated by Dirk Zimmer. New York: Dial, 1983.

Harper, Wilhelmina. *Ghosts and Goblins.* New York: Dutton, 1936.

Haviland, Virginia. *North American Legends.* New York: Collins, 1979.

Helfman, Harry and Elizabeth. *Strings on Your Fingers: How to Make String Figures.* Illustrated by William Meyerriecks. New York: William Morrow & Co., 1965.

Heuscher, Julius. *A Psychiatric Study of Myths and Fairy Tales.* Springfield, Illinois: Charles C. Thomas, 1974.

Hoke, Helen. *Spooks, Spooks, Spooks.* New York: Watts, 1966.

———. *Witches, Witches, Witches.* Illustrated by W. R. Lohse. New York: Watts, 1958.

Ikeda, Hiroko. *A Type and Motif Index of Japanese Folk-Literature.* Folklore Fellows Communications, no. 209. Helsinki: Suomalainen Tiedeakatemia, 1971.

Jacobs, Joseph. *English Folk and Fairy Tales.* Illustrated by John D. Batten. New York: Putnam, n.d.

———. *More English Fairy Tales.* New York: Putnam, 1894.

Jagendorf, Moritz. *the Priceless Cats and Other Italian Folk Stories.* Illustrated by Gioia Fiamenghi. New York: Vanguard, 1956.

Jayne, Caroline Furness. *String Figures and How to Make Them: A Study of Cat's Cradle in Many Lands.* New York: Dover, 1962.

Johnson, Clifton. *The Oak-Tree Fairy Book.* New York: Dover, 1968.

Kavcic, Vladimir. *The Golden Bird: Folktales from Slovenia.* Illustrated by Mae Gerhard. Trans. Jan Dekker and Helen Lencek. New York: World, 1969.

Kroeber, A. L. "Tales of the Smith Sound Eskimo." *The Journal of American Folklore*, Vol. XII, 1899, p. 166.

Leach, Maria. *The Thing at the Foot of the Bed and Other Scary Tales*. Illustrated by Kurth Werth. Cleveland: World, 1959.

Leodhas, Sorche Nic. *Always Room for One More*. Illustrated by Nonay Hogrogian. New York: Holt, Rinehart & Winston, 1965.

———. *Twelve Great Black Cats and Other Eerie Scottish Tales*. Illustrated by Vera Bock. New York: Dutton, 1971.

MacDonald, Margaret Read. *The Storyteller's Sourcebook: A Subject, Title, and Motif Index to Folklore Collections for Children*. Detroit: Gale Research/ Neal-Schuman, 1982.

———. *Twenty Tellable Tales: Audience Participation Folktales for the Beginning Storyteller*. Illustrated by Roxane Murphy. New York: H. W. Wilson, 1986.

MacManus, Seamus. *Hibernian Nights*. Illustrated by Paul Kennedy. New York: Macmillan, 1963.

Manning-Sanders, Ruth. *A Book of Ghosts and Goblins*. Illustrated by Robin Jacques. New York: Dutton, 1970.

Michael, Maurice and Pamela. *Portuguese Fairy Tales*. Illustrated by Henry and Ilse Toothill. Chicago: Follett, 1965.

The Mitten: A Ukrainian Fairy-Tale. Moscow: Malysh, 1979.

Pellowski, Anne. *The Story Vine*. New York: Collier MacMillan, 1984.

Pickard, P. M. *I Could a Tale Unfold*. London: Tavistock Publications and New York: Humanities Press, 1961.

Pratt, Davis, and Elsa Kula Pratt. *Magic Animals of Japan*. Berkeley, Calif.: Parnassus, 1967.

Proudfit, S. V. "The Hobyahs: A Scotch Nursery Tale." In "Notes and Queries," *The Journal of American Folklore*, Vol. IV, Jan-March, 1891, p. 173.

Ransome, Arthur. *Old Peter's Russian Tales*. Illustrated by Dmitri Mitrokhin. New York: Nelson, 1916.

Riordan, James. *Tales from Central Russia. Russian Tales. Volume One*. Illustrated by Krystyna Turska. Harmondsworth, Middlesex: Kestrel Books, 1976.

Rubrecht, August. "An Arkansas Folk Tale—'Old Ben'", *Southern Folklore Quarterly*, XXXX, No. 4, 1966. p. 342–343.

Sechrist, Elizabeth Hough. *Heigh-Ho for Halloween.* New York: Macrae Smith, 1948.

Sewell, Marcia, adaptor and illustrator. *The Little Wee Tyke: An English Folktale.* New York: Atheneum, 1979.

Sheppard-Jones, Elisabeth. *Welsh Legendary Tales.* Illustrated by Paul Hogarth. Edinburgh: Nelson, 1959.

Sierra, Judy. *The Flannel Board Storytelling Book.* New York: H. W. Wilson, 1987.

Sivulich, Sandra Stroner. *I'm Going on a Bear Hunt.* Illustrated by Glen Rounds. New York: E. P. Dutton, 1973.

Smiley, Portia. "Folk-Lore from Virginia, South Carolina, Georgia, Alabama, and Florida." *The Journal of American Folklore,* XXXII, No. 125, 1919, p. 360.

Stern, Simon. *The Hobyahs.* New York: Prentice-Hall, 1977.

Tashjian, Virginia A. *Juba This and Juba That: Story Hour Stretches for Large or Small Groups.* Illustrated by Victoria de Larrea. Boston: Little, Brown, 1966.

―――. *Three Apples Fell from Heaven: Armenian Tales Retold.* Illustrated by Nonny Hogrogian. Boston: Little, Brown, 1971.

Thompson, Stith. *Motif-Index of Folk-Literature.* Bloomington: Indiana University Press, 1966. 6 vols.

Tongue, Ruth L. *Forgotten Folk-Tales of the English Counties.* London: Routledge & Kegan Paul, 1970.

Tresselt, Alvin. *The Mitten: An Old Ukrainian Folktale.* Illustrated by Yaroslava. Adapted from the version by E. Rachev. New York: Lothrop, Lee, & Shepard, 1964.

Undset, Sigrid. *True and Untrue and Other Norse Tales.* Illustrated by Frederick C. Chapman. New York: Knopf, 1945.

Wickes, Frances G. *Happy Holidays.* Chicago: Rand McNalley, 1921.

Williams-Ellis, Amabel. *Fairy Tales of the British Isles.* Illustrated by Pauline Diane Baynes. New York: Warne, 1960, 1964.

Withers, Carl. *The Tale of a Black Cat*. Illustrated by Alan Cober. New York: Holt, Rinehart & Winston, 1966.

Zelinsky, Paul. *The Maid and the Mouse and the Odd-Shaped House*. New York: Dodd, Mead, 1981.